Film, Faith, and Cultural Conflict

FILM, FAITH, AND CULTURAL CONFLICT

The Case of Martin Scorsese's
The Last Temptation of Christ

Robin Riley

Westport, Connecticut
London

Library of Congress Cataloging-in-Publication Data

Riley, Robin, 1952–
    Film, faith, and cultural conflict : the case of Martin Scorsese's The last temptation of Christ / Robin Riley.
       p. cm.
    Includes bibliographical references and index.
    ISBN 0–275–97357–3 (alk. paper)
       1. Last temptation of Christ (Motion picture)   I. Title.
    PN1997.L3443 R55   2003
    791.43′72—dc21   2002193044

British Library Cataloguing in Publication Data is available.

Library of Congress Catalog Card Number: 2002193044
ISBN: 0–275–97357–3

First published in 2003

Praeger Publishers, 88 Post Road West, Westport, CT 06881
An imprint of Greenwood Publishing Group, Inc.
www.praeger.com

Printed in the United States of America

The paper used in this book complies with the Permanent Paper Standard issued by the National Information Standards Organization (Z39.48–1984).

10 9 8 7 6 5 4 3 2 1

In memory of my mother, Donna Lee Riley

CONTENTS

PREFACE

The premise of this book is linked to a rather simple proposition about human nature and behavior. We all blame someone at some time, for something for which we are unwilling to take responsibility. We readily place blame on those who threaten our ideas and beliefs. We conveniently label them with tags such as "liberal" and "fundamentalist." On these victims, we place our failings and shortcomings, thereby alleviating our anxieties and renewing our sense of purpose. Scapegoating enables us to transfer our failures to others and continue living, guilt free.

In this framework, the researcher cannot escape the domain of the rhetorical. His words are implicated in the shared activity of blame. Still, it is common for academics to view the object of study in terms of what we ourselves do not lack; we often fail to make the connection between the lack that we observe in others and an existential condition shared by all. We view ourselves as the source of the missing component that will correct the situation or solve the problem. Although I partly agree with this orientation, the element "lacking" could also be viewed as a condition of denial existing within the researcher. In other words, as objective researchers we tend to deny in ourselves the presence of the flaw we find in others. As a mode of criticism, scapegoating allows me to present issues and constituencies from within the broader cultural configuration, as a participant in the highly contextualized conflict over meaning construction. By adopting this rhetorical voice, I am able to avoid the pitfall of evaluating subjects and persons solely in terms of what *they* lack. In other words, I present arguments here as one who admits his tendency to blame.

This book examines a largely unrecognized process, scapegoating, as it shapes the arguments and controversy surrounding the film, *The Last Temptation of Christ*. It observes in these arguments a common mechanism of blame and examines the activity of cultural scapegoating for the purpose of increasing our collective understanding and improving human relations among competing views. "Getting along with people," Kenneth Burke observed, "is one devil of a difficult task, but that, in the last analysis, we should all want to get along with people" (*Attitudes* xi).

My purpose is to educate readers but, at the same time, I do not place a great deal of confidence in the view that more knowledge will bring about meaningful solutions. For the most part, more information will not enable us to avoid future conflicts of this nature. What *we* lack, and so dearly need, is self-examination and introspection. These reflexive processes have the potential to invigorate democracy and increase levels of tolerance.

The orientation adopted by this monograph is partly the result of an inability to separate personal issues from the issues being studied. In this respect, the treatise represents my internal struggle to reconcile liberal and conservative factions within me. The book has not resolved this tension, although it seems clear which force prevails in this particular context.

Many of the concepts and ideas presented here were inspired by scholars who have had a positive influence on my life. Among these individuals are mentors and professors from the University of Utah: Doug Birkhead, Christine Oravec, Mary Strine, Bob Avery, and Tom Sobchack. I have benefited greatly from studying with these individuals along with those who have made a valuable contribution to my theological education: Bill Herzog, Dwayne Christensen, Quentin Schultze, Michael Russo, and Michael Morris. A number of colleagues have provided valuable feedback on the book's content and I want to thank Terry Lindvall, James Crocker-Lakness, Gene Roble, and Chris Koford for their incisive comments. I am also grateful to my family, who have been an important source of support over the years of research and writing. I am particularly indebted to my sisters Tara and Elizabeth along with brother Bob and brother-in-law Tim Buchanan for their contribution to my development. I am especially grateful to my mate, Bonne, for her friendship and love.

Chapter 1

INTRODUCTION

The controversy surrounding Martin Scorsese's 1988 film *The Last Temptation of Christ* was one of the most prominent episodes in the recent history of popular culture to challenge fundamental beliefs about the sacred. The film arguably generated more conflict, controversy, and public debate than any other movie in film history, igniting a wide range of deeply felt emotions about issues and values. For a short time, Scorsese's religious movie was on the minds and lips of millions of Americans as they debated the legitimacy of the film as an expression of free speech and as an expression of the Christian religion. These segments converged around felt threats to fundamental life stances and those beliefs and ideas held most dear.

The *Last Temptation* affair is reexamined here as part of a rhetorical process in which questions about fundamental relationships between secular and religious domains were brought to the surface of cultural consciousness. It is reconsidered for the way it reflects deep levels of social and cultural insecurity produced by the shifting role of religion and religious language in a secularized society. The controversy surrounding the film demonstrates how a popular film about Jesus captured, inflamed, and strengthened existing animosity between the religious conservative community and liberal progressives. The outcome of the *Last Temptation* affair reveals a somewhat altered social landscape, one in which both secular and religious forces have reintegrated each other's view as a ritualized form of evil—a victim. Evidence to this effect suggests that the *Last Temptation* affair contributed to a general loss of the reconciliatory exigencies of social discourse. The cooperative aspects and common ground of debate over such areas as religion and popular film have eroded. As a result, both of the main social segments involved have become more reliant on scapegoating as a primary element in the formation and maintenance of their identities. This study examines how competing social hierarchies blamed and victimized one another in a contest over social and filmic space. Beyond this, it demonstrates how media texts themselves contribute to the production of new forms of scapegoating; that is to say, how a secular culture transforms and reinstitutes religious processes and rituals in secular language and images.

SCAPEGOATING, A CONTEMPORARY RITUAL OF BLAME

Scapegoating involves a "system of accusations whereby opposing views identify a common threat and label it as the enemy" (Girard 12). This study adopts René Girard's premise, that the mechanisms of religious scapegoating underlie all cultural conflict (*Things Hidden* 18). Girard argues that scapegoating is a mimetic process that repeats itself in cycles of social conflict initiating victimization, rituals of redress and cultural amnesia (114). In his discussion of Burkean thought, C. A. Carter suggests that scapegoating is a "characteristic of human life, the act by which an insecure person raises his or her own sense of self-esteem by lowering the status or attacking the confidence of someone else" (9). In this battle for legitimacy, Carter argues that "the higher seek to control the lower for reasons other than those of efficacy, namely for reasons of self-justification" (9).

The principle function of scapegoating is to legitimize and validate social hierarchies—integrated value and belief structures that are developed, sustained, and renewed through conflict. Social hierarchy is a moral configuration having sacred mandates and sanctions at its core. Almost any group or segment of society can be thought of in terms of social hierarchy, whereby members retain their standing by following prescribed rules of membership. The scapegoating mechanism performs a special function in social hierarchy. It allows for a ritual cleansing of guilt through the identification of violator and violation (C. A. Carter 18). In scapegoating, the victim is transformed into an object of blame whereby the group expunges sin and guilt. As a result, the power and legitimacy of the group is validated even as they are reformulated anew.

Carter examines scapegoating as a master concept for the Burkean socio-linguistic philosophy. In his study of human motives Burke confirms the enduring influence of scapegoating on human communication. The scapegoat "represents the principle of division" in that persecutors use it to "separate themselves from their own uncleanness" (Burke, *Grammar* 406). In this chronology of scapegoating a breach in the existing balance occurs, instigating an exchange between competing social hierarchies.[1] Negotiations break down as the polemical strategies become highly charged with the language of blame through which a transfer of guilt is initiated. As a result, the cultural landscape is reconfigured and new boundaries are constructed, "representing a purified state of dialectic opposition to the sacrificial offering" (406).

In order for such animus to appear on the cultural radar screen significant provocation must occur. When a substantial level of antagonism is generated, as is the case with the *Last Temptation* controversy, unification among opposing segments is produced (Girard 86). Here the "common threat" appeared as a popular film that prompted religious conservatives to mobilize against Universal Studios and the film's director in defense of their sacred beliefs about Jesus Christ. In the two-way play of blame, the defendants responded by labeling the religious attackers as "radical fundamentalists" and by targeting all stripes of Christians involved in the protest with a polemic of blame. The opposing positions, discussed here as liberal progressives and religious conservatives, polarized against one another in a contest over social terrain and cultural legitimacy. The two constituencies became locked in a struggle for legitimacy, attacking the weakness of the opposition while reaffirming their own institutional legitimacy. In the process of scapegoating these antagonistic voices attempted to sway public opinion to their side and thus renew and strengthen the authority of their cultural mandates. Promulgated in the wake of the crisis, persecution and victimization guide the group's behavior and insures its survival (86).

According to this way of thinking, "blasphemy" was the first alarm sent to rally religious conservatives, activating defensive processes. "Censorship" was the same forewarning for liberal progressive advocates of First Amendment rights. In the war of words and ritualized behavior of alienation the enemy is turned into an object of ridicule and mockery through public demonstrations of dominance (Girard 210). The faults and failures of the persecuting group are then transferred to the enemy, imposing a condition of guilt on the victim. Scapegoating, as a cultural process, requires judgment and punishment, which are assessed in terms of language, and images communicated. In the signage of conflict whereby blame is understood as a rhetorical transfer of guilt. The tangible indicators of punishment take the form of public ostracism characterized by the language of shame and humiliation.

Believing in the guilt of their victims, perpetrators of scapegoating are polarized by the enemy who, in a process of victimization, is perceived to be part of an ominous power having resources to destroy society itself (111). Calling on their sacred texts and eternal verities, each segment justified its rhetorical and symbolic acts of resistance to the perceived threat. Seeing this threat in only the most stereotypical ways, each social hierarchy emerged to defend itself and reclaim its legitimacy as shaper of American society.

Locked in a rhetoric of blame, neither of the two prominent positions involved in the *Last Temptation* controversy would acknowledge the processes underlying their rhetorical activity. Each segment publicly blamed the other for the faults and problems facing American society. Universal executives and Martin Scorsese considered their views to be tolerant and open-minded, even as religious conservatives claimed they were being blamed and victimized by the film. Likewise, there is no apparent awareness on the part of the liberal progressive defenders of the film of any complicity in the victimization of religious conservatives. Following a logic of scapegoating, the film's defenders saw religious conservatives themselves as the origin and sole cause of the problem (22). In their view, the problem lay with the "Bible-toting fundamentalists"; therefore, any persecution of religious conservative beliefs was justified, even necessary, to insure the safety of free speech. Denial of culpability and the transfer of guilt strengthen scapegoating as a cultural system of protection (6). Through it, competing groups maintain their unity and their identities are reinforced and confirmed.

Scapegoating, as René Girard suggests, is initiated at times when boundaries between distinct cultural segments are blurred or diminished. The *Last Temptation of Christ* affair demonstrated this blurring of formal boundaries between secular entertainment and conservative Christian religious doctrine. For example, the film blends Christian religion with secular concepts in a merger of religious piety and escapist entertainment. Its significance, in this sense, was that it eliminated differences between two distinct and opposing cultural entities (22). Ironically, in this merging of secular and religious worlds, a Hollywood film studio donned the symbolic mantle of religious authority previously reserved for Christian institutions. Universal disputed the religious and theological arguments coming from conservative Christians by making its own religious claims about Jesus Christ. The unlikelihood of this position can be ascribed to what Girard refers to as "the free operation of scapegoating

where all methods are employed for the purpose of inventing an enemy"
(6). To confirm this point the study cites a number of documents that
argue the film's protesters were misguided and wrongheaded.

Most scholars and film critics who supported the film also denied it
was offensive by separating the film's meaning from its effect (7). Chapter 3 points out that the film, by its very nature, conceals the forces of
persecution embedded within the film itself. The chapter demonstrates
how scapegoating is at work within such concealment and denial. "Persecutors," as Girard would identify perpetrators of scapegoating, deny
the film was offensive and ascribe blame for the controversy to the
protesters themselves while providing no reasonable explanation for
the strength or magnitude of the popular resistance generated by the
film (7).

As this work shows, scapegoating has altered and transformed the
relationships among these participants. This study observes that the
breakdown of formal boundaries between secular and religious domains
precipitated by the affair marks to a gradual loss of confidence in mutually accepted cultural processes of reconciliation. Likewise, the collapse of mutual respect for the opposing view is examined as part of the
more general abandonment of unifying beliefs among disparate constituencies. The general loss of unifying language is, in part, attributed to
a phenomenon of scapegoating embedded within the discourses of competing hierarchies. Scapegoating, as an organizing principle, pivots on
each group's survival needs and is ignited by perceived threats to the
group's identity.

According to Girard, "there are few cultures that do not subject their
marginals to certain forms of mistreatment and ridicule" (18). American
culture is not unique in this regard. But as the *Last Temptation* controversy demonstrates, there is little or no recognition on the part of those
involved, that scapegoating is a formidable influence in cultural formation and maintenance. Scapegoating is "deceptive, since the persecutors
are convinced that their violence is justified" (6). One purpose of this
research is to increase awareness of the prevalence of cultural scapegoating and its formidable role in the ongoing transformation of American society. This study argues that scapegoating is used in American
culture broadly as a legitimate and potent mode of social correction. It
offers credible evidence that scapegoating is an enduring process that has
the power to shape and transform a society. The effects of scapegoating
are evident in post–*Last Temptation* America, where the moral landscape
has been altered as a result of its implementation.

The scapegoating associated with the *Last Temptation* affair has hardened the boundaries between competing social hierarchies and weakened the common bonds connecting them. Religious conservatives have become more embattled and marginalized as a result of the conflict. Their social currency in entertainment media and film has diminished substantially. Likewise, the Christian Church's traditional role as America's moral compass has diminished or removed from these communication media in the years proceeding the film's release.

Correspondingly, the ideals espoused in the Constitution and First Amendment have lost credibility among religious conservatives who believe the modernist ideals of American democracy have compromised the moral code that, in their view, gave it life. Liberal progressives have become increasingly alienated from the moral code of Christianity as a result of scapegoating. Likewise, the trusting relationship long maintained between the film industry and the public has been altered and delegitimized.

OVERVIEW OF THE BOOK

Scapegoating is applied here as a method for uncovering the arguments and rituals produced by a variety of groups and individuals as they defend distinct and competing interpretations of the film, *The Last Temptation of Christ*. As a framework for rhetorical analysis, the scapegoat motif is also used to analyze specific texts and examine the relations of power between opposing social hierarchies in American society. Social hierarchy is used here in accordance with Burke's definition, as "the motive of the sociological order, made possible and necessary by social differentiations and stratifications due to the divisions of labor and to corresponding distinctions in the possession of property" (*Religion* 41). Scapegoating works within these stratifications of power and as "moral strivings" among competing segments (41). The film provides the polarizing ingredient around which these hierarchies gather to reconfirm and renew their cultural mandates in the face of firm resistance.

The texts examined in this study (language, films, and television programs) are viewed as the productive, semiotic materials that give currency and definition to events of the day. They are treated as the symbolic base from which meaningful generalizations are formed. These texts uncover mechanisms by which liberal progressives and religious conservatives dealt with hostile conditions and formative challenges to foundational beliefs. Of particular interest are the negative forms of rhetoric that constitute the discourse of scapegoating, that relationship between social hierarchies (religious conservative and liberal progressive), the production of guilt and the linguistic purgative of scapegoating (Reuckert 203). This study works across genre and media comparatively to discover similarities and differences in the polemical mechanisms and to analyze those factions producing them.

Following the controversy through its life cycle, this study examines prominent developments for changes in the relationship between the two primary groups studied: religious conservatives and liberal progressives. These groups are formulated on the basis of their common historical position concerning the film's meaning and significance along with the rhetorical strategies these groups used to support their interpretations in the face of strong disagreement. In a framework of scapegoating, the social networks and quasi-religious alliances are organized around accepted positions regarding the film's meaning and significance.

Patterns of antagonism, which developed as a result of the film, are examined initially in chapter 2, which provides a narrative reconstruction of the affair covering a period of about sixteen months. This narrative is developed from the examination of historical materials including letters, news stories, advertisements, promotional material, and biographical treatments. These materials are used to compile a record of important events concerning the film, its production, release, and reception.

Chapter 3 takes up the film's controversial story line and examines its unique conception of the sacrificial victim, Jesus. Starting from the assumption that every Christ film is a complex narrative of scapegoating; this examination opens up the film's unique formulation of persecution and victimization. Its story line, content, characterizations, and production values are examined as contributing forces in a polemical document. It finds that the *Last Temptation* presents a particular unorthodox formulation of the Christ story and a unique presentation of its sacrificial victim, Jesus. This formulation of the Christ story is studied as a rebuttal to traditional Christian treatments and as a representation of liberal progressive values and beliefs.

The analysis of the film precedes a more localized and specific exploration of the communication between competing parties over the film's meaning. Chapters 4 and 5 inspect the textual material and language produced by these antagonists and the polemical strategies present in the materials. The two competing interpretations of the film coming from religious conservative and liberal progressive are categorized according to their positions on the film's meaning and legitimacy as a work of film art. These two chapters also, to some degree, document the changes produced in the relationship between these social hierarchies and are used to evaluate the roll of religious language in sustaining and legitimizing the arguments for and against the film. Chapter 4 argues that scapegoating is embedded within the polemical documents and communication produced by religious conservatives. In an exchange with the film's producers, the chapter opens a study of the religious conservative concerns and their attempts to derail the film's production and distribution. It examines the gradual collapse of negotiations with Universal Studios and the intensification of their attacks on the film using highly emotional and polarizing language.

Chapter 5 examines the arguments and language put forward by the film's defenders. Defending it as an embodiment of free speech, the film's supporters were unified in support of the film as protected speech. The statements of film reviewers and critics are examined. This chapter investigates how Universal's defenders resorted to distinctively religious ideas and language to protect the studio and often applied the strategies used by religious conservatives to produce counterclaims about the film's religious meaning and significance. Of particular interest is the inflammatory and emotional language that, in many ways, mirrored the highly charged emotional language of those they opposed.

Oprah Winfrey's feature program on the topic offers an opportunity to examine the process of scapegoating through the lens of a commercial television. Shifting to the arena of television talk, this portion of the work focuses on the program's position supporting the film as a document of free speech. Parsing Winfrey's use of audience feedback, production values, and guest appearances, this portion of the study finds that Oprah delegitimized the concerns of religious conservative Christian guests. Beyond this, it finds that the talk show recruited scapegoating through a spectacle of conflict for the purpose of insuring audience involvement. It shows how rituals of blame are perpetuated in commercial television program content and production values.

Three legal cases brought against the film are discussed in chapter 7, which assesses the language in these legal rulings as the concluding phase in the process of blame. This chapter is particularly focused on the way court rulings reproduced forms of blame through codified forensic language and legal proceedings. It concludes that the failed legal attempts to stop the film's exhibition mark a completion of a process of blame whereby religious conservative concerns were denied legitimacy. It observes that the secular language of legal discourse reincorporated the language and rituals of scapegoating, strengthening its role in legal and moral conflicts.

NOTE

1. My categorization of the two competing orientations is constructed around mutually accepted points of contention. Liberal progressives are primarily identified in terms of their resistance to and dislike for those who opposed the film. Likewise, religious conservatives are identified in terms of their uniform dislike for Hollywood's treatment of the Christ story. These categories provide very useful ways to consolidate segments of the population that polarized in opposition over the film's contents and meaning.

Chapter 2

HISTORICAL DEVELOPMENTS IN THE *LAST TEMPTATION* CONTROVERSY

Placing the *Last Temptation* controversy in historical context provides a clearer understanding of the breadth of the conflict and range of involvement by various segments. This chapter provides a narrative explanation of the *Last Temptation* affair and documents changes that occurred over the period of 16 months, beginning with the film's acceptance as a project at Universal Studios and ending with film's release on video. Key developments in the cultural dispute are sewn together through a rhetorical model of cultural alienation and scapegoating. The historical instances captured along the way weave certain distinctive qualities into the narrative. Key players are featured as they struggle over challenges to their positions and respond to events at hand. Two major constituencies emerge from this conflict: religious conservatives and liberal progressives. These alliances rose out of felt threats to sacred paradigms—those texts held most dear. Deeply rooted insecurities were sparked. Fears and anxieties came to the surface, disclosing themselves in forms of retribution and blame. Processes of scapegoating played out in various public arenas and media.

Social conflicts such as the one that attended the release of the *Last Temptation* require rebels, heretics, and visionaries who ignite the fire of social discontent. Scorsese's religious vision put on the screen is a rebel's vision. One may also say that it is his status as a heretic that ignited both his personal mission to produce the *Last Temptation* and the public debate that erupted over its meaning. Scorsese's controversial religious vision came about as a result of the fusion of two disparate worlds he sought to reconcile—film and religion. His statements and claims reinforce the idea that Scorsese saw himself as an outsider in both of these worlds, a marginal figure who sought some form of recognition and thus a kind of reintegration and reconciliation with these social segments. By making a Christ film, he would resolve the tension between these worlds and achieve a sense of spiritual fulfillment. "I felt that maybe the process of making this film would make me feel a little more fulfilled" (Scorsese 122). His deep inner longing for spiritual fulfillment is constantly referred to in biographical statements and quotes.

The *Last Temptation* controversy can be traced back to Martin Scorsese's personal religious convictions and his desire to make a spiritual film that expressed his convictions. While filming *Boxcar Bertha* in 1972, Barbara Hershey gave him a copy of Kazantzakis's novel, and Scorsese became convinced that the book would provide the foundation for his religious work. The novel gave him important and useful ideas about how he might produce an alternative view of the cinematic Jesus, one that stressed Jesus' humanity. In 1977 he visited Kazantzakis's widow, Eleni, and convinced her to release to him the film rights to the book (Kelly, *Journey* 162).[1] Years later, in February 1983, Scorsese announced he was going to produce *The Last Temptation of Christ* based on a script by Paul Schrader (Broeske 6.1). His producers would be Robert Chartoff and Irwin Winkler, who had produced *Taxi Driver* and *New York, New York*. For Scorsese, the *Last Temptation* became a personal obsession; it represented his desire to immerse himself in a work that would provide him with spiritual illumination.

Scorsese approached Paramount Pictures with Schrader's screenplay hoping for financial support. He explained to studio executives that he wanted to make a religious movie about Jesus (6.1). The parties entered into extensive contractual negotiations and concerns over a script that was deemed "too dark." Studio executives approved a low-budget production in 1983. By September the film had been cast, a shooting schedule of 100 days was set and a budget of $16 million was approved (120). Preproduction activity moved into action and locations were scouted.

Christian activists took note of the Paramount negotiations and, when the agreement became public, quickly began developing forms of resistance. A group of Protestant women called the Evangelical Sisterhood heard that Paramount was making a movie of Kazantzakis's *Last Temptation* and in the June newsletter asked people to protest (Kelly, *Journey* 174). Angry letters of protest poured in to the Paramount offices. By the end of the year, the studio was receiving 500 letters a day, around 5,000 a week, all requesting that the film not be made (Oney G1). Barry Diller, chairman of the board of directors, confronted studio executives asking, "Why am I getting five hundred letters a day? What are we doing here?" (Kelly, *Journey* 177).

In the face of such growing resistance, studio executives became more cautious. In an attempt to dissipate the tension Paramount agreed to sponsor a theological discussion of the film and invited representatives from prominent religious persuasions to participate (Scorsese 175). The seminar was affirming of the *Last Temptation* project but did not allay fears or solve the problem of public suspicion. Thousands of letters poured in (Oney G1).

The Diller reaction indicates that studio executives were not generally aware of the book's controversial nature. They were, however, highly sensitive to the religious reaction. Executives at the parent company, Gulf & Western, heard about the controversy, both through emotional letters and from within organizational channels (Oney G1). Religious objections concerning the content of the film began to have an effect on the studio's position. Then, around Thanksgiving both producers resigned from the project. At about the same time the studio executives had a change of heart, concluding that the risk was clearly not matched by the film's potential for profit. Nor was the studio able to make the film more appealing and less controversial—especially as Scorsese gave no indication that he would compromise his religious convictions. Less than a month before shooting was scheduled to begin Paramount canceled production.

In spite of the successful resistance spearheaded by a small group of religious conservatives to halt production, Scorsese and his supporters would not give up on the project. Scorsese unsuccessfully pitched the project to Universal, Warner Brothers, New World Pictures, Hemdale, and Carolco. Discouraging as this was, Scorsese continued to search out every possible funding source, which included some rather unorthodox tactics. One idea that surfaced involved an attempt to make the film with the assistance of the French government that regularly awarded grant money to artists seeking support (Broeske 6.1). But when Scorsese's film was brought up as a possible candidate for this aid, French conservatives campaigned against it (Oney G1). The Archbishop of Paris, Cardinal Lustiger, delivered a warning to French president Mitterrand not to support a project that "subverted the Holy Scriptures" (G1).

In another unsuccessful attempt, Frixos Constantine, a Scorsese supporter with Russian influence, sought money from Moscow (G1). When that showed no promise, shooting in Greece was then discussed but was abandoned as well. Scorsese's agent Harry Ufland continued to sell the idea to potential backers, but had no success. The project had associations of conflict and scandal that were unappealing to potential funding sources. Finally Scorsese dropped the project to take on other work. He later recalled his feelings about the canceled project. "It was as if someone had died. But I really had a sense that God was with me on this film. And when we had to stop, I figured God was telling me I just wasn't ready" ("Director," *Newsday* 11).

The project sat dormant for three years until Scorsese signed on with Michael Ovitz and Creative Artists Agency in 1987. By this time he had become known as an innovative new director of films including *Taxi Driver* and *Raging Bull* (G1). Scorsese pitched the project to Universal's new president, Tom Pollock, explaining that he wanted to make a sincere religious movie about Jesus (Scorsese 40). Scorsese's passion for the subject was compelling and Pollock worked out an agreement. One author notes that the studio was not interested in Scorsese's personal agenda, or *Temptation,* but thought that if it funded his personal art film maybe someday Scorsese would produce a successful film for Universal (Keyser 169). Scorsese was offered $6.8 million and 58 days to complete the Moroccan shoot. Such financial and scheduling constraints would have been the end of many projects, because a comparable film would require at least $20 million and a 70-day shoot. Scorsese agreed and proceeded to gather a cast and skeleton crew for the production. Shooting started in October 1987 and a rough cut was scheduled to be completed by July 1988.

Scorsese's religious mission came out in every aspect of the production, where he facilitated a kind of spiritual/religious reenactment of the New Testament story. Indeed, the thrust of the film's central theme, "the normal life" lived by a God, captivated the cast who, for the most part, spoke of the shoot as a transformative experience. They enthusiastically participated in the journey of isolation to experience the "way of the cross." Stories of self-depravation and self-denial punctuate the accounts of the shoot. On more than one occasion crew members talked about the production of the *Last Temptation* as rife with problems—a nightmare. The remote location, the intense physical demands of the desert shoot, the lack of normal comforts of Western settings, the limitations of personnel and equipment, exposure to the harsh environment of the Moroccan desert, and a shortened shooting schedule, made it extremely demanding for actors and technicians (Kelly 203). Michael Ballhaus, the cinematographer, commented, "It was almost like war. We had to have a plan for every shot. We were counting minutes" (211).

Such conditions allowed Scorsese to come as close as possible to replicating the actual experience of Jesus and his disciples in order to induce spiritual initiation and awakening. The more suffering the better, because the film could then take on the realistic look Scorsese sought. The crude life of the Moroccan desert stripped away all distractions and all news about the uproar developing at home.

RESISTANCE TO *TEMPTATION* GROWS

Word spread through the Christian community that the film was in production, and once again conservatives mobilized in force. Letters were sent by the thousands to MCA, Universal's parent corporation, who hired Tim Penland of Christian Marketing to act as a liaison between the studio and Christian community. "I'm hopeful they will be able to embrace a film that shows the human side of Christ yet affirms Christ as Savior," says Penland, "But if the movie is blasphemous, or if Christian leaders feel it would be damaging to the cause of Christ, that will be the end of my involvement with this project" (Poland 43). Penland was a key figure for religious conservatives, who maintained close contact with him during his work with Universal. Among these leaders were the Rev. Lloyd Ogilvie, a well-known local Presbyterian pastor; the Rev. Bill Bright of Campus Crusade; the Rev. Donald Wildmon, head of American Family Association; and Ted Baehr of *MOVIEGUIDE*. Penland provided this network of Christian leaders and organizations information about *Temptation* as it moved through the pre-production phase. Penland, however, was not provided inside information about the film and had not seen the rushes or read the screenplay. When a pirated Paul Schrader script surfaced in April 1988 and was circulated among Christian leaders, Penland had no knowledge of its contents. The early script was the first hard evidence that Scorsese was going to adopt the controversial ideas presented in Kazantzakis's novel. Shock waves rippled through the religious conservative community.

Material in the script inflamed the anger of evangelical church leaders, who made hundreds of copies and sent them to churches and media organizations across the country (48). In his reflection on the screenplay Poland observed, "Everybody who got a copy must have made at least a dozen copies and distributed them. Some heads of denominations sent copies to every one of their ministers" (49). One scripted phrase that became well known was Jesus' saying to Magdalene in the dream sequence, "God sleeps between your legs" (Schrader, Screenplay 82). Another passage involved Jesus confessing to a compatriot his misgivings about his status as messiah: "I'm a liar, I never tell the truth," and "Lucifer is inside me" (51).

Although some of the material from the draft is not included in the final shooting script, it made no difference to conservative Christians. They cited the screenplay as concrete evidence of the director's malice and the studio's deliberate deception about the film. Like a bull seeing red, the militant wing of the religious conservative arm of Catholic and Protestant churches mounted a formidable demonstration of protest through letters, phone calls, and boycotts, using the script to successfully lobby public support and inflame public opinion.

Penland read the screenplay, was incensed, and resigned his consulting position with Universal in June. Poland reflects on a joint sense of betrayal: "It wasn't a big deal to Tim or me that we had been ripped off in a premeditated assault by the top executives of a giant American corporation. In all fairness, we asked for it. We calculated from the very first that we might be being set up by Universal for its own nefarious purposes" (201). The pirated script made any reconciliation between the two, Universal and religious leaders almost impossible and effectively set the stage for an all-out battle between the studio and the Hollywood community and religious conservatives of all types and affiliations.

The studio sent out a release denying claims about the pirated script, asserting that the final script was not inflammatory. Studio head Tom Pollock asserted that the early conservative reaction was a result of misinformation (Kelly 236). The statement seemed to add more fuel to the blaze and religious conservatives became more and more convinced that the pirated script was a good representation of what would be in the film. The studio's ongoing attitude toward religious conservatives was, at best, veiled hostility and, at worst, outright defiance.

Initially it was religion that motivated the project and religion that killed it. Paramount's decision to halt the production was caused by a direct campaign of well-organized religious conservatives. Universal faced the same kind of religious pressure but responded by moving in the opposite direction. In contrast to Paramount, Pollock and Universal consistently defended Scorsese's religious integrity and artistic vision. The pressure from religious conservatives seemed to stiffen Universal's protection of Scorsese and his project. As the tensions built the studio even played on the controversy, promoting *Temptation*'s much anticipated release with greater vigor and energy.

When Universal decided it would not respond to the massive resistance, the film's meaning and significance changed dramatically. The film then was pushed to the center of a public debate over religion and a larger battle against perceived censorship of free speech.

Reactionary conservatives viewed the film as a breach in normal social behavior and as a refusal to honor Christian beliefs about Christ. They felt victimized and humiliated in part because they could not imagine their sense of self apart from the high esteem given Jesus. By publicly challenging their view of Jesus, Universal unilaterally bound religious conservatives to forms of retaliation. When viewing the matter from this frame of mind, it follows that blasphemous acts had to be met with retribution, as we find here, in a highly stylized rhetoric of scapegoating in which the violator is shamed into compliance (Miller 8).

A network of Christian organizations poised to launch the most extensive and scathing attack against a movie in recent history. A broad-based coalition of Christian organizations, denominations, and churches united behind the ancient banner of blasphemy.[2] Fueling the protest were organizations like the American Family Association, a conservative Christian organization that monitors Hollywood. The AFA sent out 2.5 million pieces of mail in a matter of days to arouse awareness and support. Other like-minded organizations, including *Focus on the Family,* Jerry Falwell's *Old Time Gospel Hour* and Family Radio Corporation, churned out negative communication about the film in order to lobby resistance to its release. In one of his mailings Wildmon attacks the studio, "For MCA/Universal to spend millions of dollars to put the lie on a movie screen and arrogantly say that 'Christians will not stop us from distributing this film' is intentionally insulting." Wildmon continues, "MCA/Universal is saying to all of Christendom: 'So what if you are insulted. We care nothing about your feelings. So what if it isn't based on scripture or even the spirit of your scripture. We care nothing about your Holy Scripture' " (Editorial 1). Wildmon's statement is characteristic of the evangelical response—deeply felt personal offense. It also manifests the conservative moral vision itself, one of strength, unity, and power—single-mindedness against a serious threat to sacred beliefs.

Conservative leaders were told by Universal back in February that they would be allowed to see the film well ahead of its planned release and their input about it would be taken seriously (Dart, "Church Leaders" 1). When the studio postponed the screening, Wildmon, Bright, and others took it as another tactical move by the studio to avoid facing them and dropped their plans to attend (Poland 68). Universal responded by arguing it had not gone back on its promise of the advanced screening and said it planned to reschedule one within seven days of its receipt of the film (Dart, "Church Leaders" 1). Universal wrote Wildmon urging restraint, saying Scorsese's film would "serve as a reaffirmation of faith to Christians" (1).

CHRISTIAN DENOMINATIONS ADOPT STRATEGIES OF RESISTANCE

While religious conservatives argued they were being provoked, many Christian organizations and denominations did not feel the film was a sufficient threat to warrant such reactionary measures. To these "mainline" denominations the film was not unduly threatening. Presbyterians, Lutherans, Methodists, some American Baptists, United Church of Christ members, and Episcopalians maintained, for the most part, a neutral posture and sought to mediate between extremes neither embracing the film nor arguing against it. Bill Fore, head of the umbrella organization for the mainlines, the National Council of Churches, went on record stating that the protest was off-target (Dart, "Church Leaders" 11). Fore's comments reflect the view of leaders of mainline denominations who were open-minded about the film's religious value. Robert E. A. Lee, the head of Lutheran Film Associates felt the film could promote healthy dialogue about the humanity of Christ (16). Martin Marty, Evangelical Lutheran Church in America's professor for modern church history at the University of Chicago, commented that there is no noncontroversial way to portray Jesus' humanity, implying that perhaps the controversy demonstrated a healthy surfacing of theological and doctrinal issues (Lee 17).

In contrast to the alarmist view of religious conservatives, the mainline churches were primarily concerned about how the film might divide the church and its parishioners. Many produced advisory statements: "Use your own discretion," and urged calm. The Office of the Bishop of the Evangelical Lutheran Church in America made a statement that it " . . . does not advise its members whether they should or should not attend individual films" (17).

A great divide separated these "progressives" from their more conservative Catholic and Protestant brethren, who uniformly agreed that the movie was a deliberate attack that could not be ignored. The National Association of Evangelicals, the umbrella organization for five major denominations (some Baptists, Holiness-Pentecostals, Anabaptists, Reformed and Independent Fundamentalists), released a formal statement urging Christians not to see the film (17). In a *Christianity Today* editorial, Terry Muck argued that evangelical protests were an appropriate way for Christians to exercise their freedom of speech and that such films warranted a variety of protest strategies (14).

The Rev. Donald Wildmon and his American Family Association organized a plan to picket theaters and boycott MCA products. Millions of letters were sent to sponsors of programs produced by Universal Pictures to urge advertisers to take a moral stand against the studio (Reilly). In these letters and other correspondence, Wildmon described the film as a "blasphemous, evil attack on the Church and the cause of Christ" (1–3). Other prominent ministers joined the chorus. Among these leaders were the Rev. Lloyd Ogilvie of Hollywood Presbyterian, Pastor James Kennedy of Coral Ridge Church, the Rev. Jack Hayford of the Church on the Way, and Dr. Bill Bright of Campus Crusade for Christ who used his extensive channels and connections to fuel the protest. "We'd like to make this the last temptation of Universal to make a film that is going to defame the name of Jesus Christ (Dart, "Church Leaders Upset" 3).

One of the most vocal of the clergymen and also perhaps the most openly criticized was the Rev. R. L. Hymers of the Fundamentalist Baptist Tabernacle of Los Angeles, whose rhetoric was particularly inflammatory, accusatory, and anti-Semitic (Bruning 9). Hymers led a small contingent of followers to picket the home of Lew Wasserman, head of MCA (Universal's parent corporation). The demonstrators burned Wasserman in effigy, invoking the Jewish scapegoat strategy. Media coverage of the event alarmed liberal progressives who were incensed by such callous acts.

During the summer months of June and July the uproar intensified, drawing other groups into the debate. Numerous religious organizations made formal statements concerning the film, generally condemning it. Billy Graham issued a press release calling the film "sacrilegious" (Billy Graham Ministries). Larry Braidfoot, general counsel for the Southern Baptism Churches, stated that the film was offensive "because it portrays Jesus as indecisive and uncertain, and Judas as heroic" (Dart "Full Theaters" 1.1). Pat Robertson of the *700 Club* voiced his concerns, as did Paul Crouch of Trinity Broadcasting. Jerry Falwell and his *Old Time Gospel Hour* advertised "battle plan" press kits for the active protester (Bravin 10). Radio personality and psychologist James Dobson of *Focus on the Family* used his network of 250 radio stations to blast the studio and its director. "Scorsese and Universal are not merely taking on evangelicals; they are taking on the King of the universe. God is not mocked. I don't know how long it will take him to speak, but he will speak" (4).

Others from the conservative ranks were forthright in their condemnation. Morality in Media head Joseph Reilly judged the film to be an "intentional attack on Christianity" (10). The American Society for the Defense of Tradition, Family, and Property (ASDTFP) published a full-page "open-letter" to Universal Studios in the *New York Times* with the word "Blasphemy" across the top of the page (A7). The text of the letter states, among other things, that Universal was defaming Jesus Christ, who should be protected from such acts by law. The film's apparent challenge to Jesus' divinity was the primary force that mobilized millions of Christians. The force of mass-mediated communication, combined with highly complex communication networks and structures within the church communities, produced a formidable response to the studio's plans to release *Temptation.*

Catholics were divided on the topic, but the U.S. Catholic Conference supported the protest and came out with a statement condemning the film as "morally offensive" (Goff 8). Bishop Anthony Bosco, spokesman for the Office of Film and Broadcasting, criticized the film's morality and gave the film its most objectionable rating "O" (Morton 33). Cardinal Joseph Bernardin of the Archdiocese of Chicago chimed in with his disapproval of the film as well (Goff 8). Mother Angelica of Eternal Word Television Network, a Catholic cable channel that had access to 11 million cable subscribers, spoke against the film, saying, "It jeopardizes our faith" ("MPAA Supports" 3). Numerous archbishops from various cities also became involved in orchestrating protests of various kinds.

At this historical juncture in the conflict there were few voices favoring moderation and dialogue. Instead, both positions had solidified their support and were waging a war of retaliation and blame, corrective strategies for avoiding further public humiliation and embarrassment.

The number of Universal supporters swelled as the controversy gained national press exposure. Free speech advocates took the rhetorical position that a film could not offended anyone. These progressives pointed out that movies are fantasies occupying space outside our day-to-day reality—escapes from reality concerns. By adopting this position, reviewers, commentators, and film critics could separate the film's cultural significance from its relevance as free speech—in effect, denying any provocation had ever occurred. The power of such scapegoating resides in the official denial that a normative social behavior has been violated (Miller 20). William Miller points out that in situations in which scapegoating surfaces, certain forms of domination and economic exploitation are allowed to take place under the guise that there is no domination at all, only beneficence and amicability (20).

UNIVERSAL HOLDS ADVANCED SCREENING

In an attempt to diffuse the growing controversy, or play on it for publicity, Universal went ahead and screened the film in New York on

July 12 for a select group of religious leaders who might be supportive of the film's message (Dart, "Some Clerics" 11). The guest list was, in religion writer John Dart's words, "a tip-off." Those in attendance included representatives from organizations critical of the religious right, including Fundamentalists Anonymous and People for the American Way (11).

Approximately 30 church leaders, Protestant and Catholic, attended the screening of the two-hour and 38-minute rough cut. Their responses were generally supportive of the film's message. Paul Moore, an Episcopal bishop, had a positive reaction. "I saw nothing blasphemous in it" (Dart, "Some Clerics" 11). The Rev. Robert L. Maddox, a Baptist minister and official with Americans United for Separation of Church and State, was even more affirming, "The overall impact was powerful on me. When I was a pastor, I preached that, I felt Jesus really did have those struggles" (Dart, "Some Clerics" 11).

Bill Fore, head of communications for the National Council of Churches, used the occasion to criticize religious conservatives: "It's a shame that some Christians appear to be so unsure of their faith that they can't stand the thought of people seeing something different" (11). The Rev. Eugene A. Schneider, deputy director for the office of communications for the United Church of Christ, said *Temptation* was a film that "raised compelling questions about faith and the nature of divinity," although he found it to be boring (Gorney D1). United Methodist Communications film producer and critic, Kathleen LaCamera, endorsed the film's religious themes, commenting, "It's powerful to show that Jesus was both human and divine," noting that his human side is often forgotten (3). Echoing these thoughts was a prominent Catholic clergyman and author, Father Andrew Greeley, who wrote an article supportive of the film saying, "Although Mr. Scorsese's Jesus is not the Jesus of the scriptures, the film makes us think about God" (22). These moderates were not threatened by the film and did not view it as an attack on their religion. It simply represented one of many interpretations within a diverse religious cultural milieu.

Some of the attendees, however, did not care for Scorsese's view of Jesus. Bishop Anthony Bosco, head of U.S. Catholic Council Communication Committee, spoke in a cautious tone about the film. "I believe Scorsese has failed to treat the topic well. . . . As it is, the film is flawed both as theology and as cinema" (Morton 33). The film was even less popular with Evelyn Dukovic, executive vice president of the conservative watchdog organization, Morality in Media. She reported back to the organization that the film "intentionally demeaned Christ" (Dukovic, "Report" 2).

The refusal of other key religious conservatives to attend the preview resulted in a complex series of events that fueled accusations on both sides, and the fact that most of those organized against it had not seen the film became one of the more enduring points of criticism of their argument. Penland, Poland, Bright, and Wildmon initially planned to attend the preview. It was not until the pirated script surfaced and the preview date changed that these leaders pulled out of the arrangement. Two other factors influenced their decision not to attend. According to Poland, attendance could in itself be interpreted as a sign of endorsement—providing a form of justification to the studio. Second, to view a film that debased Jesus was interpreted by these conservatives as a willful sin against God. These conservative leaders felt the film's content could very well affect a viewer's faith in a negative way. Still other factors cloud this preview event. For example, the Rev. Jerry Falwell's invitation to the screening was revoked by Universal because he criticized the film before seeing it. Apparently Falwell agreed not to comment until after the viewing ("Falwell's Invitation" 13D).

On the same day that Universal previewed the film to a select group of religious leaders, religious conservative organizers held a well-orchestrated press conference at the Registry Hotel in Hollywood denouncing MCA and Universal for their lack of sensitivity. The news conference was held in the same room where a year before Pope John Paul II asked leaders from the entertainment community for understanding and compassion in the presentation of Christian values. Universal chairman Lew Wasserman hosted the papal visit.

One year later, more than 120 members of the news media came and listened to Evangelical leader's objections to Universal's planned release and distribution of the film (Broeske 13). The group outlined its specific objections to Scorsese's film adaptation of Kazantzakis's novel in formal statements. The Rev. Lloyd Ogilvie called the film "the most serious misuse of film craft in the history of movie making" (Broeske 13). The Rev. Jack Hayford likened the depiction of Christ in the scripture to a caricature and said "it was as if George Washington was portrayed as a combination of Benedict Arnold and Gomer Pyle" (Poland 230). For Hayford, the movie (referring to the pirated script) defamed Christ in a way that blacks and Moslems would not be allowed to be demeaned (Broeske C13). Bill Bright argued that "a handful of people with great wealth and depraved minds" were corrupting the world (C13). The thrust of their message was that, if the film was not withdrawn, they would launch an all-out boycott of MCA/Universal products and services. The group clarified that it did not advocate censorship but would like to see the film destroyed (Harmetz, "Ministers Vow" C13). Universal responded to these concerns by issuing a statement of rebuttal: "In the last few days some fundamentalist leaders have attacked the film stating clearly that their goal is to prevent its release. These individuals declined an invitation to see the film and consequently much of what they are saying is inaccurate and exaggerated. The filmmaker deeply believes that this film is a religious affirmation" (C13). Universal was showing no signs of softening its position on the film. The tone of defiance coupled with claims about the director and the film set the tone for Universal's future rebuttals of conservative concerns.

Evangelicals considered other more desperate ideas. Dr. Bill Bright offered to purchase the film from Universal. In June 1988, Bright devised a plan whereby he "would be personally responsible for reimbursing Universal for the amount already invested in the movie" (Poland 123). The overture was to become more an act of provocation than a sincere proposition. Bright's offer was sent in a letter to the studio; a copy was also presented to the *Los Angeles Times*. Bright's plan was to acquire the film and destroy it.

Universal lashed back by publishing its refusal to sell the film in full-page newspaper ads in the *Los Angeles Times,* the *Atlanta Constitution, Variety,* the *Washington Post,* the *Hollywood Reporter,* and the *New York Times.* The ads explained why the company had no intention of allowing the movie to be held from theaters. The studio claimed the film was both a legitimate form of religious expression, a sincere attempt to produce an artistic film about Jesus, and "a work of fiction . . . a personal exploration" (Universal C30). In the unusual defense of its own picture, Universal used its newspaper ad to reprint the content of Bright's letter. Universal placed itself at the forefront of religious warfare—fighting the foes of free religious expression. "In the United States no one sect or coalition has power to set boundaries around each person's freedom to explore religious and philosophical questions" (Universal Studios Advertisement).

Growing press coverage of the dispute in the summer of 1988 aroused the interest of leaders in the Hollywood community, including members of the Screenwriter's Guild, the Actor's Guild, the Director's Guild, the major studios, reviewers, and critics. These groups, for the most part, took up Universal's cause. Jack Valenti, president of the Motion Picture Academy Association, issued a statement in support of Universal and booked visits on television talk shows where he refuted the religious conservative arguments. In his mid-July release Valenti attempted to quell rumors that Universal might buckle under the pressure and not release the film. "The major companies of MPAA support MCA/Universal in its absolute right to offer to the people whatever movie it chooses" (Harmetz, "Top Studios" C18). Pat Buchanan provided a terse editorial response to Valenti that is reflective of the growing polarization between interpretations of the film's meaning: "The reason Universal and Scorsese are doing this is because they know they can get away with it. Their Hollywood chums will whisper, Right on! Stick it to-em!" (A9). Joseph J. Reilly, head of Morality in Media, called Valenti the "chief carnival barker for American films" after debating him on the *Today Show* (6).

During the course of these developments Scorsese made numerous appearances and statements to defend his film and clarify his intent. Many such statements included references to personal faith and the belief that the Jesus in his film is the Jesus of the New Testament. "He resisted temptation because he came to terms with his own nature, the divine nature" (Scorsese 117). Religious conservatives did not believe Scorsese and lambasted him as a heretic and blasphemer. In an editorial Rev. Donald Wildmon wrote, "Mr. Scorsese could not accept the Jesus of the Bible, so he created a god that he could accept" (*AFA Journal* 3). In his book on the controversy, Rev. Larry Poland refers to Scorsese as a "dark director" preoccupied with the sinister side and incapable of producing anything with goodness in it (43).

In mid-July, religious conservatives still felt they had a chance to halt the film's release if enough resistance from the public and press could be brought to bear on the studio's position. The efforts to bring about an acceptable resolution became more unlikely when Universal announced it would change the release date from mid-September to mid-August. In the surprise move Universal announced it would release the film six weeks early, moving the exhibition date to August 12. Tom Pollock's statement to the press on August 4 explains the studio's reasoning: "As Universal has said before and will say again and again until someone begins listening: Our position in this is that we are backing Martin Scorsese's vision. . . . It is his movie—we are doing this for him. . . . And in the end it will all come down to the movie. And the movie will speak for itself" (White B1).

The change in the film's release date prompted religious conservative strategists to move into high gear. Rev. Larry Poland and David Moore, director of communication for the Los Angeles Catholic Archdiocese, planned a second press conference at the Registry Hotel in Hollywood set for August 9, three days before the *Last Temptation*'s release. At the meeting, 10 prominent Christian leaders from a wide range of denominational backgrounds called for "an all-out boycott of MCA/Universal"[3] (Poland 132).

Although they were unable to force Universal to withdraw the film from release, religious conservatives were quite successful in pressuring a number of theaters and chains not to show the movie. Petition drives in numerous states gathered tens of thousands of signatures, which were then sent to theater owners and legislators. Fact sheets were disseminated widely, urging Christians to boycott all businesses owned by MCA if the company released the film. Christian talk-radio announcers induced more reaction from listeners and generated intense telephone protest campaigns both to Universal and to theater conglomerates.

These demands produced a growing reluctance among theater chains to book the film. J-F Theaters, Inc., which operated more than 60 screens in the Baltimore area, refused to show the film. Vice President Tom Herman stated his reason; "Right now I would say there are about 10,000 letters in my office. Does this tell you what's happening? " ("Three Local Movie Chains" 2). General Cinema, the fourth largest American theater chain with 1,338 screens, announced it would not book the film. Loew Theaters and Carmike Cinemas also disclosed their refusal to run the film on any of their 1,200 screens ("Loew Giveth" 5). Mann Theaters, with 447 screens owned by Paramount, identified the controversy as its reason for not running the film (Modderno 8). A spokesman for the 1,200-screen United Artists Theaters said, "It's not worth it for any theater chain to play a film like 'Temptation' that will offend our regular customers" (8). In Southern California, the Edwards Cinemas of Newport Beach, with dozens of theaters, reported they would boycott the film (8).

Bill Soady, president of Universal's distribution division, argued that exhibitors were "rushing to judge a movie without giving it a fair shake" (8). Still, movie chains continued to take a position against the film. Bill Spencer, whose 320-screen Moyer group included theaters in small Northwest towns, was skeptical of *Temptation*'s appeal outside major cities: "This is one film exhibitors will not book unless they are absolutely sure the movie will make tons of money in its initial limited release" (8). Luxury Theaters of Portland, Oregon, was added to the list not showing the film (Chandler 1).

In an attempt to reassure those concerned about censorship, Universal vice president of national field operations, Sally Van Slyke, issued a release assuring the public that there was no cancellation by chains that booked the film, and *Temptation* would open on 1,200 screens nationwide (Harmetz, "'Last Temptation' Opens" 13).

The Screen Writer's Guild, alarmed by the cautious position adopted by theater chains, took out a full-page advertisement in trade publications asking exhibitors to rethink and reverse their policy of not screening the film: "The guild believes that the decision of certain exhibitors to withhold a film from national and regional exhibition because of the opposition of a few highly vocal groups ill-serves the interest of art, the industry and the democratic society which allows both to flourish" (Dawes, "Loew Giveth" 5). The guild threw their full weight behind Universal and Scorsese in the fight against what they viewed as a fringe of fundamentalist censors.

Even though religious conservatives were influential in the film's cancellation by major theater chains, they were not able to force Universal to halt its plan for the *Last Temptation*'s exhibition. They organized one final attempt to stop the film's release, a public rally set for August 11, the day before the film's national opening, at Universal's "Black Tower" headquarters in Los Angeles. The protest, organized by Los Angeles Christian media, brought out an estimated 25,000 people (Hirsley, "L.A. Christians" 5). The throng of believers gathered carrying wooden crosses and placards with messages such as "Coming Attraction: Judgment Day at Universal" and "Scriptures, Not Scripts!" (Hirsley, "L.A. Christians" 5). Donald Wildmon addressed the crowd: "We're launching a movement! Christian bashing is over! The time when Hollywood can ridicule our faith and our values and now even our God is over!" (gesturing to the headquarters building in the background) (Poland 192).

Jane Chastain, spokesperson for the Concerned Women of America, told the rally audience that the film's release was a deliberate fueling of the controversy for profit: "We find Universal's First Amendment argument as a mandate for releasing this film an insult to the intelligence of the American people. . . . We are appalled that a company like Universal Studios would distort anyone's religion for the purpose of making a profit" (193).

Jewish and Muslim leaders also made statements at the rally. They saw a common enemy in Hollywood exploitation. Rabbi Haim Asa of Orange County and local Jewish leader Dennis Prager of KABC also addressed the rally. Prager labeled Universal as a nihilistic exploiter of Christian values: "Christians should have understood long before 'Last Temptation' that nearly everything that their religions hold sacred had been profaned in the movies. The issue is not Christian censorship; it is Hollywood nihilism" (Chandler 1). Muslim spokesman Dr. Maher Hathout read a statement: "Human decency and ethical standards should keep all people respecting each other's religions" (1).

The rally appeared to be a success with protesting conservatives and the local media gave extensive coverage to the event, some of which spread to the national level. Universal's offices were inundated with phone calls and mail for days proceeding the protest. On a single day, 122,000 letters were received (York 1). Nevertheless, the carefully orchestrated event did not convince Universal to cancel the film's release.

The next day, August 12, high-profile members of the Director's Guild of America publicly voiced their unqualified support for the film and Scorsese's artistic vision at a press conference at the headquarters in Los Angeles (Hirsley, "L.A. Christians" 3). In attendance were Tom Pollock, Peter Bogdanovich, Billy Wilder, John Carpenter, Oliver Stone, Robert Zemeckis, James L. Brooks, Martha Coolidge, Randal Haines, Penny Marshall, George Sidney, Elliot Silverstein, and Warren Beatty (3). Beatty appealed to the public for support of Universal and Cineplex Odeon, "in their effort to resist pressure groups and to encourage studios to continue to finance and distribute material that is not so safe" (Harmetz, "LT Opens" 11). Clint Eastwood, who was not in Los Angeles at the time, sent his comment: "Freedom of expression is the American way" ("Brouhaha" 5). In addition, their formal press statement argued that, "it should be the individual's right to decide for themselves what they will see and think" (Hirsley, "L.A. Christians" 3). Throughout the strife and conflict, Scorsese himself insisted he was directing an acceptable movie about Jesus. A story in the morning *Los Angeles Times* featured his comments: "It represents my attempt to use the screen as a pulpit in a way, to get the message out about practicing the basic concepts of Christianity" (Broeske 6.1).

The film was released that evening. An ad campaign promoting the film read:

"MARTIN SCORSESE, AMERICA'S MOST GIFTED,
MOST DARING MOVIEMAKER,
MAY HAVE CREATED HIS MASTERPIECE."
Richard Corliss, Time Magazine
On Friday, August 12,
one of the greatest filmmakers
of our time brings us a startling vision.
An extraordinary story,
based on the highly acclaimed
novel by Nikos Kazantzakis.
THE LAST
TEMPTATION
OF CHRIST

(Universal C30)

Universal ran accompanying advertisements in Los Angeles, New York, Washington, and Atlanta that likened the protests to the historic "burning of books."

TEMPTATION OPENS UNDER HEAVY PROTEST

Because the film had so few bookings it opened to packed houses and tight security in nine U.S. and Canadian cities: New York, Los Angeles, Chicago, Seattle, Minneapolis, Washington, D.C., San Francisco, Montreal, and Toronto. Many in attendance admitted they bought tickets simply to counter the protest efforts of conservatives to prevent its release (Dart, "Full Theaters" 1.1). Ticket sales soared; receipts averaged between $40,000 and $50,000 a theater, a better per theater average than the action thriller *Die Hard* (Harmetz C14). Relieved by the response, Pollock went on record claiming victory over the forces of censorship. "We're gratified at the response of the American people" ("Opponents Undeterred" 14).

Throngs of protesters were outside theaters demonstrating peacefully while policemen and security guards looked on. The first two weeks of the film's run produced minor incidents and clashes between hostile parties. At the Los Angeles premiere a man stood up in the middle of the film and shouted, "This film is blasphemous," while others told him to "shut up" (1). In the same showing, when the director's name came up in the credits there were cheers and applause (1). At its debut in Manhattan around 100 demonstrators shuffled around in front of the theater singing songs and hymns such as the "Battle Hymn of the Republic" (1). In Chicago the most identifiable group picketing were Greek Orthodox members who could be heard shouting, "Stop the blasphemy" and "Jesus Christ was not a sinner" (1).

There were a few incidents of vandalism, disruption, and violence. Police were called to Scorsese's daughter's home August 23 to investigate a suspicious-looking package (Wright 28). The parcel turned out to contain a rock and letter critical of Scorsese's film (28). A Commonwealth theater in Pine Bluff, Arkansas, was victim to a "Temptation" protester, who set fire to the building (Quinn 23). In a Southern California mall a scuffle broke out between security guards and Christians protesting the film's exhibition ("Scuffle Breaks" 12). Apparently, demonstrators ignored repeated requests by security to leave their picket signs outside the mall in Santa Ana. Counterprotesters carried banners proclaiming the right to free speech and expressed support for Universal and Scorsese.

At the film's premiere in Salt Lake City on August 31, a print of the film was stolen from the Cineplex Odeon Theater where vandals had slashed the screen. A second print was made available and the viewing went on two hours late (Dawes, "Stolen Prints" 8). That same weekend *Temptation* opened in the South, where protest rallies were conducted (Dawes 8). Christians in Action of Dallas followed through with its plans to have a "peaceful and prayerful protest" when the film arrived. An estimated 2,000 people showed up at the downtown theater (Dawes, "Peaceful, Prayerful" D3).

In Atlanta, Archbishop Eugene Marino called the 2,000 demonstrators to a day of prayer and fasting. Seattle had similar numbers when the film opened there to mostly peaceful protests and rallies in support of positive views of Jesus (30). Organizer Robert Dalgleish, president of the Family Values Alliance of Seattle, along with local Christian radio stations, organized protest pickets. Hundreds of demonstrators walked in front of the downtown theater where the film was being shown. The Seattle Catholic community objected to the film and the archbishops asked that Catholics not patronize the movie (Ostrum G1). All of the negative attention brought curiosity seekers and First Amendment supporters pouring into theaters.

After months of unsuccessful attempts to keep the film out of theaters through letters, press conferences, correspondence, protests, and boycotts, conservatives turned their attention to the government, hitting local, state, and federal officials with a barrage of letters and phone calls. Two congressmen were responsive and took up the cause and addressed the issue on the floor of the House of Representatives. Representatives Robert Dornan of California and Robert Hubbard from Kentucky on separate occasions went on record with statements blasting Scorsese and Universal Studios (Congressional Record H6970 and E3433). Hubbard argued that the studio was taking advantage of the protest to gain box office receipts. He called it "a shrewd marketing ploy." He went on, "One difference between Judas Iscariot and Martin Scorsese is that Mr. Scorsese will earn more than 30 pieces of silver from his betraying Jesus Christ" (H6970). New York Governor Mario Cuomo, in an interview with WMAC public radio in New York, said he would ignore the film. "Bad taste is allowed in our society. But as you are free to exercise bad taste, I am free to ignore you" ("Film Offensive to Cuomo" C19). Alabama Governor Guy Hunt made public reference to the film stating that he hoped it would not be shown in his state.

Many municipalities drew up resolutions against the film.[4] Others attempted legal action against MCA/Universal. Veda Nayak asked that the

U.S. District Court for the Southern District of Texas enjoin the distribution and presentation of the film by a Houston Cineplex Odeon theater there ("Fifth Circuit Dismisses" 1). The courts ruled against her. The Escambia County Commission in Pensacola, Florida adopted an ordinance banning the film that was overturned (Tortorano). The District Court judge ruled to enjoin the enforcement of the ban because of clear conflicts with the First Amendment (Levy 532). In Pennsylvania, Michael Greb filed suit against Universal and exhibitors in Pittsburgh, arguing the film ridiculed his religious beliefs ("U.S. Supreme Court" 1). His suit was dismissed by the district court, the state appellate court, and finally at the Supreme Court.

In a similar attempt in Massachusetts, the Rev. Curtis Rowe of Heritage Baptist Church of Springfield invoked eighteenth-century blasphemy laws in his protest against the film's exhibitors (Bazinet 1). The outdated law could not be enforced and he dropped his suit. In addition to these actions, the film was banned on at least one college campus—the Oklahoma State University Board of Regents voted to suspend the film's showing ("Oklahoma State University" 2).

Reviewers and critics varied in their analysis of the film but were consistent in their condemnation of the protest. Generally these liberal progressive supporters of the film downplayed the protest while congratulating Scorsese on his great religious vision.

News programs, talk shows, and various other media venues picked up the topic and debated the issues as well. The *Oprah* program sponsored a religious debate on the film as did talk-oriented shows *Morton Downey, Jr.*, and CNN's *Sonya Live*. *Nightline* discussed the issues, as did *Crossfire* and *MacNeil/Lehrer News Hour* (Kaye 17). Oprah Winfrey, for example, used the affair to discredit conservative Christians and cast aspersions on their concerns. Downey, Jr. went even further in attacking conservatives as money-grubbing opportunists. The scope of the protest and underlying issues were left largely unexamined.

As the controversy raged in the United States, other regions of the world also debated the film's merits. In Britain, the National Organization of Viewers and Listeners considered the film to fit within the ancient British blasphemy laws and rallied against it (Dawes, "L.T. Touches" 5). The British Film Board cleared it for release in England and Scorsese attended its London premiere (8).[5]

Its reception was not so peaceful in France. At the film's September 28 opening in Paris, violent demonstrations broke out (Nayeri 23). At the UGC Odeon in the Latin Quarter, assailants attacked the entrance to the theater amid a rally of praying demonstrators. The attackers broke windows and lobbed tear gas canisters at the entrance (Nayeri 23). French resistors, in many cases led by Catholic clergy, assaulted theaters in several cities and towns, throwing firebombs, rocks, eggs, and tear gas. Thirteen policemen were injured in the Paris demonstrations alone and one theater was burned to the ground. In the face of persistent tear gas and incendiary attacks, five Paris theaters dropped *Temptation* after its first week (Nayeri, "Paris Sites Drop" 481).

Religious Italians were also uncomfortable with having *Temptation* shown at local theaters (Dawes 13). The Roman Catholic Archdiocese of Venice asked that the movie not be shown at the upcoming Venice International Film Festival (Spring 1989). This position was reinforced by well-known film director Franco Zefferelli, who was one of the few among Scorsese's peers to strongly denounce the film. He threatened to remove his entry in the festival if Scorsese's *Temptation* was shown (Nayeri 481). Zefferelli called *Last Temptation* "a deliberate operation to create controversy . . . a terrible film, vulgar and obscene, offending the most important personage in the history of mankind" (Robbins 6).

In Kazantzakis's homeland of Greece, where the book had caused a stir some 30 years earlier, the film was not well received; Greek Orthodox priests and their followers protested at several cinemas in Athens. The Opera cinema was ransacked, and the screen was ripped apart with knives. The thousand or so protesters ruined projection equipment and seats were also torn. Riot police were sent out in full force and had to use tear gas and nightsticks to hold the unruly crowds at bay ("'Temptation' Protest Leads" 481).

In South America, Brazilian Roman Catholic clergy actively protested the film. President of the National Conference of Brazilian Bishops D. Luciano Mendes-de-Almeida compared Scorsese's film to AIDS: "One does not have to be contaminated by AIDS to be against the disease" ("Uncertain Future" 8). In Australia, the state of Queensland Censorship Board banned the film while it went into theaters in other states without incident ("Oz Censors Lower Classification" 481).

Over the next few months—October, November, and December—the film made its way into film houses across the country. At its January 12 premiere in Fargo, North Dakota, about 50 demonstrators braved the subzero temperatures to voice their disapproval ("Demonstrators March"). When the film finally made it to Coeur d'Alene, Idaho, the first audience was evacuated because of a bomb threat, which turned out to be a hoax ("Protests, False Bomb Threat Over Movie" Wire 1). The incident is an appropriate postscript to the film's tumultuous life.

By February 1989 the major events of the controversy had come and gone and the critics, reviewers, and commentators were turning their attention to other matters. The film had made its way through theaters in Europe and around the world. Universal released *Last Temptation* on home video in July 1989, without store displays, promotional posters, or advertising ("'Last Temptation' Released . . . " B2). MCA Home Video President Robert Blattner provides a suitable epilogue to the social drama: "We were conscious of provoking a new controversy, which was clearly not in anybody's interest" (Quoted in "'Last Temptation' Released" B2). Blockbuster, the nation's largest video store chain with 343 company-owned outlets, refused to carry the video (B2).

In the aftermath of the protest, some religious conservatives thought their efforts had an economic impact. Rev. Wildmon claimed that the protests and boycotts caused Universal $10–12 million in losses (Voland 6.2). Statistics from the *Daily Variety* conflict with this, however, showing *Temptation* had slipped through with a bit of a profit, grossing nearly $8 million at the box office and $4.2 million in domestic video rentals (2). Overseas, *Temptation* grossed about $4 million by February 1989. Wildmon had speculated that the film cost the studio $15 million, but reliable sources indicate that the figure was actually closer to $10 million (Poland 2). These figures indicate that Universal has made a small profit on the film.

DEFINING THE FUNDAMENTALIST RESISTANCE

Much has been said about the religious advocates of the protest, some in a balanced manner, but most sources provide inadequate information. For example, sources commonly overlook, or fail to acknowledge, the number of people involved and the groundswell of Christian support given the protest.

Analysts of the conflict differ in their examination of this broad-based religious alliance. News organizations following the events commonly identified those protesting the film as "Christian fundamentalists." This label is also the most prevalent description among scholarly works and historical treatments. It is fair to say that "fundamentalists" actually were the single largest block of protesters, but the range and scope of those involved went far beyond this small group to include more moderate organizations and those that cut across denominational lines.[6] Protesters of this kind included mainstream Christians numbering in the tens of millions. These corporate groups, factional quasi-religious groups, and ego-centered networks of leaders bridging denominational boundaries formed a patterned response led by clerics and factional leaders.[7]

CONCLUDING REMARKS

The genesis of the *Last Temptation* conflict resides in a combination of factors that have been discussed here. First among them is Scorsese's determination in having the film made and Universal Studio's willingness to back him in the face of tremendous resistance. The fact that the studio stood by him and financed the film as a favor to him became a factor in generating more controversy. Second, there was an almost immediate response by Christians to perceptions of violation in emotionally charged and reactionary resistance. Third, religious conservative protests expanded across the country in attempts to keep the film from being released. They declared themselves victims of a concerted campaign to impugn their sacred figure and mounted a retaliatory campaign against the director, the studio, and the film industry.

The film reignited underlying tensions between religious and secular constituencies. Opposing segments within society formed, solidified positions, and engaged in a pitched contest over what could, and what could not, be publicly said about the historic figure of Jesus. Film critics were talking about God and religion as were studio executives, directors, commentators, actors, movie producers, movie critics, and film exhibitors. The rhetoric of these positions became more adversarial and confrontational as the drama played out. By July 1989 religious conservatives had lost the battle, although it is not entirely clear what Universal had won.

NOTES

1. Sidney Lumét was the first filmmaker to acquire rights to the novel from Kazantzakis's widow in 1971. Lumét, however, never cast the film nor did he produce a screenplay.

2. The scope and size of the religious conservative response is discussed at the end of this chapter, but a rough estimate of those involved, Catholic and Protestant, comes to around 40 million people.

3. In attendance were Tim Penland, consultant for Universal and mediator; Mother Angelica of the Catholic television network ETN; Bill Bright of Campus Crusade; Father John Bartke of St. Michael's Orthodox Church; Sister Rebecca of the Evangelical Sisterhood of Mary; Bishop John Ward, auxiliary bishop of the Los Angeles archdiocese; Thomas Wolf of the Southern Baptist Convention; and Robert Ziener, the national chairman of Rosaries for Peace.

4. Some local authorities sympathized with the protesters. Houston Chief Deputy Constable Glen Cheek ordered that all deputies under his jurisdiction could not work off-duty security jobs at movie theaters showing *Last Temptation* (McDonell D3).

5. Scorsese made a brief statement to the press at the event: "If you feel you will be offended by the film, don't see it. But please allow others to go." Two years later the BBC would drop its plans to screen the film (Johnston 1).

6. Fundamentalists adhere to a literal interpretation of biblical scriptures maintaining their validity as truth and to the idea that such truths give believing persons their identities and value.

7. Kosmin and Lachmans's National Survey of Religious Identification shows there are an estimated 12 million conservative, or very conservative, Roman Catholics (15). The National Association of Evangelicals represents around 50 denominations, 42,000 local congregations with over four million members. It includes a wide variety of denominations such as the Assemblies of God, the Free Methodists, and the Salvation Army (295). The Southern Baptist Church, a conservative organization, comprises 15 million adult members (292). Another of the larger groups involved in the protest activity was the Pentecostal Church, which has about two million members (301).

Chapter 3

DEMYSTIFYING THE
CHRISTIAN SCAPEGOAT

To a large extent, the *Last Temptation* gained its infamy and notoriety from its content. It was content that reviewers and film critics focused on and content that infuriated religious conservatives. Even today views are deeply divided on the film's meaning and significance. This chapter reopens the discussion about the film's message and provides new insights into its religious content and cultural consequence. As a complex cinematic document of blame, the film is of great value for understanding the forces at work in American society and how certain religious ideas are legitimized through filmic representations. Beyond this, it is useful for explaining how social segments convert collective guilt into rhetorical forms of cinematic blame.

Every Christ film is a complex narrative of scapegoating, in which an ancient religious story is played out in a cinematic Passion play. As ritual reenactments of the New Testament Gospels, Christ films embody a system of accusation and blame through their story lines, production values, and characters. This is not to say that all Christ movies are the same. Each embodies its historical context, the technical innovations of the times and the artistic style of its director and contributors. All Christ films do, however, adopt the formal narrative process of scapegoating as their underlying principle. As enduring religious rituals, Christ films convert collective societal guilt into forms of blame in a ritual cleansing of guilt. Christ films operate as vehicles for the transfer of this blame to appropriate sacrificial victims, thus reaffirming and renewing the foundational beliefs of its producers and the cultural segment they represent. How the *Last Temptation of Christ* reproduces the Christ story as a process of scapegoating provides important insights into its meaning as a rhetorical document. As this study will demonstrate, scapegoating in the *Last Temptation* serves a very different rhetorical function from the one found in other Christ films. Most notably, its sacrificial victim, Jesus, is separated from his traditional role in founding the Christian religion.

As a polemical document, the film is analyzed here from a variety of angles. Initially this chapter surveys the origins of the film and the director's stated motivation and artistic intentions, which are implicated in the film's controversial portrayal of the Christ story. The study then restates the narrative function of the scapegoat and compares the *Last Temptation* with one of its classical predecessors, the *King of Kings*. The transformation of Jesus into a particular type of sacrificial victim is documented by studying the Christ character, specific production techniques and story material. In addition, the ambiguities found in the film's content are correlated to Scorsese's stated intentions in order to elucidate the relationship between the film's offensive qualities and its rhetorical meaning as a document, which perpetrates blame.

INSPIRING BLASPHEMY

The genesis of Scorsese's unorthodox presentation of the Christ story resides in Nikos Kazantzakis's 1956 novel by the same name. The Greek author felt the orthodox church had misconstrued God and wrote the *Last Temptation* to correct what he considered false and misrepresentative ideas about the Christ story.[1] "I wanted to Renew and supplement the sacred myth . . . setting aside the dross, falsehoods and pettiness which all the churches and all the cossacked representatives of Christianity have heaped upon his figure thereby distorting it" (*Letters* 515–16). Kazantzakis felt his literary work could redeem the true Christ, but only by subverting the one endorsed by the orthodox Church. The translator and biographer P. A. Bien notes that the Greek author intended to make the savior into a reflection of his own ambiguous and conflicted beliefs, directly challenging church doctrine.[2] "The fact that Kazantzakis not only slipped into heresy but deliberately made it a keystone of his structure should give us some clue to his deepest aims" (Kazantzakis 505). In Kazantzakis's words, the intent was to produce a story that radically altered the sacrificial victim, Jesus, and thus reopen the age-old debate over Jesus' humanity and divinity (515). Kazantzakis reinvented Jesus as a messiah who evolved into a new archetypal form, one liberated from the superstition and falsehoods of the Greek Orthodox Church. Bien observed, "He [Kazantzakis] was not primarily interested in reinterpreting Christ, or in disagreeing with, or reforming the Church. He didn't just want to transform the story, Kazantzakis wanted to lift Christ out of the church altogether" (505). His goal could be achieved only by significantly altering the formal elements of the story thus transforming its sacrificial victim into a human being tormented by a vengeful God.[3] "He is without compassion; he does not trouble himself about men or animals; nor does he care for virtues and ideas. He loves all these things for a moment, then smashes them eternally and passes on" (31). Inverting good and evil, Kazantzakis presented God as the source of torment and suffering, the divine force that manipulates Jesus through a guilty conscience.

In line with these controversial machinations, Kazantzakis used stylistic devices to invert character roles and normative religious elements of the story, in effect introducing psychological instability and doubt into the Jesus character's narrative experience. He reinvented the sacrificial victim by internalizing the moral struggle between good and evil, and by focusing attention on Jesus' inner thoughts. Nearly the entire book is devoted to Jesus' personal psychological activity and to breaking down traditional narrative distinctions between good and evil, God and the Devil, and so forth. By drawing attention to aspects of Jesus' internal struggle, Kazantzakis was able to collapse the moral absolutes of traditional Christian doctrine into relativized impulses of the savior's conscience. Kazantzakis's God is the voice of mental torment located in Jesus' self-talks, "claws" coming up the back of his head rather than an externalized source of absolute truth coming down from the heavens.

Scorsese was attracted to the way Kazantzakis magnified the psychological aspects of Jesus' life and humanity and how his book emphasized ambiguity and double meanings (*Scorsese On* 228). His film adopted Kazantzakis's formula for subjectivizing good and evil through Jesus' internal (intrapersonal) dialogue. Placing viewers within Jesus' existential condition of doubt through point-of-view camera work and voiceover narration would give them direct access to Jesus' thoughts and motives, lifting Jesus out of the institutionalized cinematic form of the traditional Christ film. Following Kazantzakis's novel, Scorsese's God also would be the primary source of persecution. "God is a headache, the hound from heaven" who pursues Jesus relentlessly (Scorsese, *Last Temptation* DVD). The screenwriter Paul Schrader developed a script that emphasized this view of the God character, "God was a vicious headache that would not go away" (*Last Temptation* DVD).[4] The most controversial aspects of Kazantzakis's portrayal were attractive to Scorsese and Schrader, who wanted to complicate Jesus' role as sacrificial victim.

Viewing Kazantzakis's novel as innovative tool for his groundbreaking film, Scorsese identified with the novel's challenge to familiar and "worn" presentations he saw as unbelievable and phony (Ehrenstein 108). "Kazantzakis opened up my sense of Jesus, pushed me beyond these kinds of images and helped me decide to take more risks . . . I figure the more risks the better" (Kelly, *Martin Scorsese* 228). "Risks" refers to artistic innovations meant to bring a freshness to the story and make Jesus real to viewers. Scorsese hoped his subjectivized Jesus would generate healthy dialogue about Christ's humanity, challenging traditional views. "I wanted to use Kazantzakis' concepts to tear away at all those old Hollywood films—even though I love them—and create a Jesus you could maybe talk to, question, get to know" (Ehrenstein 109).[5] An introduction of Jesus' human nature would open the door to artistic innovation and a unique presentation of the Christ character, one that is also more socially relevant (Jensen 371). Scorsese has taken a position that his film provides new information about the Christian savior and liberates the story of its inherent ignorance and superstition (365). "I had hoped it would be the kind of film that would engender very healthy discussions on the nature of God and how the Church should change to meet today's needs" (Rensin 59).

Scorsese's motivation and stated intentions are consistent with a belief in the "social power of art" (Jensen 365). Joli Jensen argues that artists like Scorsese "view themselves as guardians" of the cultural heritage who "make society better when they critique and thereby undermine whatever dominates" (371). This faith in art as social transformer advances the idea that bad art is the cause of current confusion and misunderstanding about Jesus Christ and good art is the cure (366).

According to Jensen, in the context of art as intellectual property, the artist is given special status as "special social seers, able to recognize social truths more clearly, deeply and well than anyone else" (371). It is the artist's task to act as catalyst and cut through the mystical forms common to the Christ film and reveal the true Christ (370). In this respect, Scorsese saw himself as an important instigator of social change, bringing about new ways of viewing Jesus Christ.

Jensen's examination of the social power of art helps explain why those who produced and supported the film failed to acknowledge its offensive qualities. They saw its victimization of the traditional Christian views as a process of freeing people from what Jensen refers to as "the spell of false consciousness" (371). Scapegoating is introduced into this view of art when its logic is revealed. To claim that one has the ability to bring about positive social change by challenging the status quo indicates that the artist has taken a position of intellectual and religious superiority over those who don't share his views. If religious conservatives refused to accept his presentation of Jesus, they have no one to blame but themselves (371). As a result of this rationale, the film's victimization of traditional Christian religion is justifiable, even necessary in order to bring about positive social change.

Scorsese does not look to or recognize the effect of his film art. Nowhere in the scores of quotes and statements is there any indication that Scorsese felt in any way responsible for the film's reception. To provide such recognition would implicate him in the activity of persecution. Instead, he repeatedly claims that the film is an artistic expression of faith that will, at some point, come to be appreciated.

Persecution is hidden within the self-justifying assumptions about the purposes and transformative power of art. In terms of the process of victimization, the assignment of blame moves in the "reverse direction" back to the offended party (Girard 21). Perpetrators of blame do not look to, or recognize, the effect of their art. "Instead of seeing in the controversy a reflection of the broader process [of scapegoating] at work, it sees in the individual stereotype the origin and cause of the problem" (21).

In contrast to Scorsese's denials, screenwriter Paul Schrader, was unabashed in his criticism of traditional Christianity and drafted a script that demystified and humanized Jesus following the narrative guidelines set out in Kazantzakis's novel. His script sought to expose the traditional belief in Christ's life, death, and resurrection as a fraud. "What we know of Christianity is, in my mind, Paulism" (*Schrader* 18).[6] Using art as an instrument of social power, Schrader added his contribution to the artistic reinvention of the Christ story, one that would be provocative and challenge the status quo. "The picture was a provocation and I enjoy debate and argument. It would be very hypocritical to say that you don't enjoy it when you incite it" (139). Drawing from his personal view that Christianity is more a product of the imagination than historical fact, Schrader's script emphasized ideas that, for religious conservative Christians, contradict and directly impugn the Christian religion and its historical view of Jesus' existence, death, and resurrection.

The fact that Scorsese's Jesus does not fulfill the function of the traditional Christ character is of little consequence to Schrader and Scorsese. Likewise, the film's radical separation of Christ from his central function as a sacrificial victim was of little concern to those who supported the movie's theme, because they considered the film to be a work of original art. The rhetorical activity of scapegoating is concealed in the guise of cinematic originality and creative genius. The fact that the film challenges traditional genre films as well as victimizes any religious views that oppose its message, is almost entirely ignored.

The film is widely viewed as innovative partly because the cultural process of persecution and victimization, which are readily visible in the classics, are concealed in a modern myth of art as social transformer (Jensen 373). In the rhetoric of scapegoating, the film's creators acknowledge only the benefits of their therapeutic work, while ignoring the negative impact for those who disagree (Girard 13).

Operating on the assumption that iconoclasm has redemptive value; the film's creators were able to eliminate the undesirable qualities of the story but could not extricate its underlying principle of scapegoating. In other words, in spite of the film's radical reworking of the biblical story, its content failed to transcend an ancient structure of scapegoating that undergirds the narrative. As a result, the *Last Temptation* produces a new set of relations in persecution and victimization (12). When brought out for examination, the film's content is implicated in a process of provocation, shedding light on the ideological and religious agenda put forward by the film's producers and supporters.

SACRIFICIAL VICTIMS, HOLY AND PROFANE

The traditional Christ film tells a biblical story about persecution, victimization, and the reconciliation of humans with the supernatural in a Christian pattern of redemption.[7] There are epic struggles between the forces of good and evil, human nature and divine goodness, the Devil and God. In traditional Christ film representations of scapegoating, these narrative tensions unfold, as Jesus the outsider becomes a central threat to the religious and political institutions of his culture. He is offered a chance to abdicate his moral authority through temptation. When he refuses he is marked for sacrifice, murdered, and then converted into the religious source of divine grace by his followers. As a result of his death and resurrection, guilt for his death is transferred to a universal supernatural source of evil. The resurrection provides the central means (through forgiveness) for reconciling humans with their failures as sinful or guilty beings (Girard 19). The scapegoat operates as a source of reconciliation whereby guilt is projected onto spiritual analogs.

Traditional Christ films follow the New Testament, portraying elements of holy and profane in familiar dualisms that communicate eternal truths of the Christian religion. Through various production techniques, they present Jesus as an innocent, uncorrupted figure that has a clear and identifiable association with the divine type present in the New Testament. He is typically presented in high esteem and is given cinematic authority through a cinematic process of mystification.

Mystification, as it is used here, does not refer directly to theological components or issues concerning Christ's divinity and humanity. Instead, it provides a conceptual link between the formal qualities of the New Testament Gospels and cinematic presentations of the Christ story. It is used as a reference to the methods and techniques applied by various films to create a filmic analog for the divine. Cinematic mystification of the Christ character has been, and remains, one of the primary identifying characteristics of the Christ film. Cinematic mystification serves to heighten the audience's awareness of Jesus' role as a sacrificial victim. Stark polarities between good and evil are created to demonstrate the holiness and innocence of the victim, and the culpability and guilt of his adversaries. Holy qualities are associated with his innocence, goodness, and purity, which are culturally and historically grounded. Profane elements are identified as moral opposites of this innocent, holy figure identified with guilt, evil, and deception. The Jesus of Nicholas Ray's *King of Kings,* for example, fulfills all of the requirements for reproducing an innocent sacrificial victim; the authorities murder him, producing collective guilt (Eliade 18). Cultural guilt is allayed through the mystified resurrection event, which serves to transfer human guilt to spiritual sources in the supernatural realm where the innocent and holy sacrificial victim is made into the supernatural object of adoration. The relationship between persecutor and victim are made plain through this transfer of guilt to a universalized symbol of evil, Satan.

By contrast, the *Last Temptation* demystifies the Christ character, altering those elements which distinguish holy from profane. Its sacrificial victim is neither innocent nor holy, and fails to conform to the narrative requirements identified with the Christian sacrificial victim. In terms of the traditional prescription of scapegoating, the film reverses the poles between good and evil, breaking down the traditional function of persecution and victimization, putting the story's sacred ideas to degraded use. For example, unlike the savior of the classics, this Jesus is a human figure who shows remorse for acting improperly and offending God. His role as a sacrificial victim is ambiguous and conflicted, placing his holiness in doubt.

Traditional Christ films construct the sacrificial victim in a variety of ways, using techniques that distinguish a holy Jesus from other characters. Through mystification, filmic narratives make Jesus "obscure or mysterious" (*American Heritage Dictionary* 869). These cinematic techniques used to mystify the Christ character include, but are not confined to, camera work, dialogue, lighting, sound, music, costumes, scenes, acting, and special effects. The presence or absence of mystification in a Christ film helps explain Jesus' role as a sacrificial victim and identify the rhetorical message embedded in the narrative.

While *King of Kings* is from another era, historically bound by the techniques and styles of the 1960s, it characterizes very nicely the technique of mystification commonly found in traditional films of the genre. Nicholas Ray's presentation of Christ accentuates differences between Jesus and other characters and thus provides a visual code that sustains the narrative contrast between an evil persecutor and a holy victim, renewing the New Testament system of scapegoating.

In the selected scene, a woman has been caught in adultery and is about to be stoned to death. The woman runs down a street toward the camera past Jesus. The angry crowd follows, stones in hand. The woman falls to the ground against a wall. Jesus follows, standing between her and the crowd. "What has this woman done?" he asks. The leader of her persecutors declares, "She's been caught in adultery and she must be stoned according to the Law of Moses." Jesus then picks up a stone and walks toward the group, "Let him who is without sin cast the first stone." One of the accusers raises his hand to throw a stone but Barabbas grips his arm, keeping him from doing so. The people look at Jesus, then drop their rocks and depart. Jesus turns and approaches the bedazzled woman who looks up at him in awe. The camera views her from a high angle as Jesus' shadow falls over her, mystifying his presence. He offers her his hand; she takes it and stands up. "Where are they now who condemn you?" he asks. She looks toward her accusers who are leaving. She is puzzled by the strange and powerful man who has just saved her from death but says nothing. Jesus concludes with a reference from the New Testament, "Then neither will I condemn you. Go and sin no more." He then turns his attention away and walks over to his disciples.

The dramatic rescue of the adulterous woman from her fate evokes her gratitude toward Jesus and God. While this gratitude is not verbally stated, it is implied by her demeanor of submission and obedience. The dialogue maintains a close link to biblical language, tying the scene to its origin in the Gospel of John. Even though it does not replicate the biblical story precisely, the narrative is consistent with its historical antecedent and the scene's meaning logically flows from those meanings found in scriptures. As a result of these continuities, the sacrificial victim, Jesus, retains his mystical qualities and predictable role as a holy messiah.

King of Kings tells the story of the adulterous woman in a linear progression and the camera predictably frames the participants in static and carefully choreographed shots. The edits are lengthy and the pace is predictably slow, accentuating the objectivized qualities of the biblical story. The camera operates as an observer, documenting events and allowing the action to develop within the frame using minimal movement and angles. The musical score is somber and reverential. As he is presented as a holy and divine person, Ray's Jesus is thoroughly mystified, objectified, and otherworldly. The production techniques give the impression that Jesus is holy and has divine authority, which sanctions his intercessory act of forgiveness. Cinematic mystification enhances the contrast between divine and human qualities, allowing the scene to develop as a story about God's forgiveness.

By employing dialogue, production techniques and music that mystify the Christ character, *King of Kings* becomes a pageant of the ritual vanquishing of evil and the restoration of Christian doctrine and its hierarchical order. Jeffrey Hunter's Jesus, however uninteresting and static, is valid as a legitimate Christian sacrificial victim because his ideas and words come across to the believer as a relevant link to the language of the New Testament. The sacrificial victim in *King of Kings* can be interpreted as an entry point to the divine—Christ is an iconic figure whom viewers gaze on in hope of experiencing some mysterious blessing.[8]

The corresponding scene in the *Last Temptation* thoroughly demystifies the Christ character bringing him down to earth and making him real. The film achieves this partly by repositioning the viewer. Instead of being outside the frame looking in on the action, the viewer observes from within the psychological activity of Jesus thoughts and feelings. Voiceover narration introduces this position at the beginning of the film and it is used here in his reflective comments at the end of the scene. Demystification is further enhanced through the musical score and camera work. A faster editing pace and camera movement make the scene feel dynamic and active. The script shifts away from the familiar the biblical language and reference to the woman's sin.

When the scene begins, the woman, portrayed here as Mary Magdalene, is being dragged by her hair into an open area where bystanders wait with stones. As in *King of Kings,* Jesus observes the event and interrupts the execution by stepping into the line of fire. The action communicates a very real sense of danger and violence (when compared to the ritualized pursuit in *King of Kings*). Jesus is pelted by the stones as the crowd yells for him to get out of the way. The leader, Zebedee, tells Jesus to move away, "Don't you hear what he said idiot? Do you want to get hurt?" Jesus responds, "I don't want this." The personal pronoun "I" shifts the context from an objectified theology to an existential condition. Zebedee reacts sarcastically, "He doesn't want this. . . . Well we want it!" Asking "Why?" Jesus then receives an explanation from Peter, who tells him of Magdalene's violation of the Sabbath by practicing her trade of prostitution. Arguing with the perpetrators, Jesus picks up two stones and looks at the members of the crowd. "Who has never sinned? Who?" The crowd begins to reflect as the mood changes. Zebedee comes forward and claims he has nothing to hide. Jesus responds, "Be careful Zebedee . . . I've seen you with that widow . . . Judith. Aren't you afraid God will paralyze you if you lift that stone?" Zebedee drops the rock in frustration and walks away. The crowd disperses as Jesus embraces Magdalene in silence. The two walk away and the scene ends with a voiceover of Jesus thinking to himself, "God has made so many miracles. What if I say the wrong thing? What if I say the right thing?"

In many respects the scenes mirror one another; both tell viewers a similar story about Jesus' role in saving a woman from death by directly challenging the authority of the executioners. The two use similar camera work and talent blocking and both ask the same question concerning the woman's guilt and sentence. The *Last Temptation* differs in that it expands Jesus' lines to include the mention of specific types of sin and he confronts the main accuser with convicting evidence of his sin. The effect of this expanded dialogue is to make the issue of the woman's sin more literal and concrete and less ethereal and abstract than the dialogue from *King of Kings*. It directs the activity of guilt and blame back to the accusers, making them the focus of scrutiny. In contrast, Ray's film produces the same scrutiny without going into detail. Instead, Jesus remains above scrutiny and gives no explanation for his behavior and does not justify his position. As a result, the scene retains its characteristics as a story about universal moral principles of forgiveness and grace.

The *Last Temptation* deemphasizes the universal moral principles by contextualizing the dialogue. For example, Jesus openly confronts Zebedee about his sins, breaking through the traditional veil that separates divine from human. No longer above the fray, Jesus enters the controversy by debating the details of the individual accusers' sins. Likewise, Jesus' holiness cannot be sustained in the context of his proclamation that it is his personal motivation, not God's, that produces the intercession, "I don't want this."

Of further significance is the fact that the *Last Temptation* drops the issue of the woman's sin once she is out of danger. Magdalene displays no reverence or awe regarding Jesus' presence or behavior but instead is preoccupied with her own suffering. In *King of Kings,* Jesus' closing words to the adulterous woman finalize the activity of intercession and forgiveness, producing the effect desired, a mystification of the Christ character. Contrastingly, Jesus' closing words in the *Last Temptation* scene have him identifying God as the source of the redemptive rescue. He has no foreknowledge of what will happen next and demonstrates no unity with the source of the miracles. Jesus ponders what will happen next, unsure of himself and his behavior in a new situation.

By employing dialogue, production techniques, and shooting styles that deemphasize Jesus' mystical qualities, the scene changes the role and narrative function of the sacrificial victim. Because he has no mystical qualities, Jesus' mission becomes ambiguous and subjective. Signified as an abstract idea, God's role is limited to Jesus' self-talk, detached from eternal truths associated with Christian doctrine. There can be no cinematic conversion of guilt to innocence in Scorsese's film because the scene demystifies its Christ character and detaches him from the sacrificial type present in the New Testament story. The sacrificial victim is an entry point, not to the divine but to the psychological struggle facing every human being. Unlike the iconic figure portrayed in *King of Kings,* this Jesus reduces the religious message to an earthly circumstance, common and accessible to all.

As this example demonstrates, the lack of mystification in the *Last Temptation* raises questions about Jesus' legitimacy as the Christian savior in part because the scene produces no transfer of guilt from sinner to Jesus, making forgiveness unnecessary. Most important, the act of saving Magdalene (and others) has no moral consequence; her behavior does not change as a result of Jesus' actions. No evidence is given to show that, once free of her accusers, the unrepentant prostitute changes her behavior. While the same could be said of the woman in *King of Kings,* the contrast created concerning Jesus' holiness and divinity provides an impression that her behavior would change as a result of his act of forgiveness.

The comparison of these two films allows one to see more clearly the relationship between the content of the *Last Temptation,* its meaning as a document of blame, and the controversy it generated. The issues raised by religious conservatives were focused on the film's treatment of Christ and its radical departure from traditional Christian doctrine concerning his role as a sacrificial victim. Their concern may appear to simply review the obvious; after all, the film intended to emphasize Jesus' human qualities. But when viewed through the activity of mystification and de-mystification, one can readily see how the film's presentation of Jesus performs a rhetorical function, the rearrangement of relations between persecution and victimization. The source of persecution found in the *Last Temptation* narrative is not identified with universal spiritual defi-ciencies of the persons as in *King of Kings*. There is no change in the accused woman's behavior in *Temptation* because evil is not separated from good in terms of his perceived holiness. The persecutor behind the moral tale is identifiable as human misunderstanding itself. From this interpretive orientation, the woman's accusers were going to kill her be-cause they failed to see their own guilt and sin. Jesus shows them this truth and they withdraw on the basis of his persuasiveness. In *King of Kings,* Jesus reveals a truth as well, but the film relies on more than his reasoning ability. Mystification holds the scene together and helps view-ers see the relationship between Jesus' actions and his ultimate function as a sacrificial victim.

King of Kings reveals to viewers what the *Last Temptation* eliminates by the way it disposes of the mystical along with the knowledge that their sacrificial victim is a scapegoat, one who takes the blame for others' guilt (Girard 117). Mystification, as found in the genre classics, flags for viewers a structural relationship between human and divine, producing the type of sacrificial victim native to the New Testament. Through mys-tification the victim's innocence is established and, according to Girard, " . . . we see the injustice of his condemnation and the inappropriateness of the hatred directed toward him" (117).

In the *Last Temptation,* Jesus has no divine authority or innocence; thus, the identity of the persecutor in the film is ambiguous and largely hidden from our view through the film's demystification of Christ. Ab-sent the mystical elements the *Last Temptation* narrative places the viewer within the film's activity of persecution rather than as an outside observer. As a result of this demystification the relationship between persecutor and victim becomes ambiguous. At the same time, the activity of persecution is transformed into a subjective, psychological activity presented to the viewer as a matter of personal conscience. When the contrast between Christ and other human beings is not integrated into the film narrative through mystification, the Christian system of scape-goating collapses. In terms of the Christian message, the human condi-tion cannot be redeemed; the ritual transfer of impure source of human guilt to a holy deity does not occur because the elements of mystification and divine contrast necessary for such a transfer have been removed.[9]

JESUS WITH A SMALL J

Scorsese's film sheds elements of mystification through an array of devices suggesting subjectivization and psychological instability, resulting in a collapse of all formal boundaries separating holy from profane. By internalizing the battle of good against evil, the director changes the moral landscape and with it he removes the limits placed on filmic explorations into Jesus' soul. This interiorization of the moral struggle of good against evil is achieved through the use of production techniques such as point-of-view camera and voiceover narration that transport the audience into Jesus' mind to experience what he sees and thinks (Tatum 169).

In this innovative departure from traditional cinematic representations, Scorsese inserts specific thoughts and images into Jesus' head, thus colonizing the mind of Christ. As a result, Scorsese gains access to an area inaccessible to the Church itself, Jesus' conscience.[10] By subjectivizing the Christ figure through point-of-view and voiceover, the film effectively changes the ground rules for debating the identity of Christ. Questions about Jesus' dual nature are no longer important; now the contest centers on whose thoughts and ideas will be inserted into Jesus' mind. The rhetorical effect of these subjectivizing techniques is to scandalize the traditional filmic presentation of Christ by putting into his mind images and words that seriously limit Jesus' appeal as a universal source of redemption.

Once inside Jesus' mind, the viewer encounters a flux of confused and competing influences. They find a Jesus who expresses no outward conviction because he has no internal guiding truth, no moral compass. At one point in the film Jesus explains to Judas, "I just open my mouth. God does the talking." In another conversation with Judas, after saving Magdalene from being stoned, Jesus says, "I was full of hate when I saw them torturing Magdalene. Yet I opened my mouth and out came the word love." When he meets John the Baptist at the Jordan River for his initiation neither is sure if Jesus is the messiah. John asks, "You're the chosen one?" Jesus responds, "I don't know. (demanding) Tell me" (33). After a brief argument over who should baptize whom, John dunks Jesus.

Scorsese frames this internal tension as part of Jesus' gradual evolution into his role as savior. "The human nature of Jesus was fighting with him all the way down the line, because it can't conceive of him being God . . . " (Scorsese 124). But the metamorphosis is not compelling because Jesus' conscience never evolves or escapes from its polluted and degraded origins. While talking to a religious devotee on a hillside, Jesus confesses that he lied. "I never tell the truth. I want to rebel against everything, against God. But I'm afraid. You want to know who my God is? Fear."[11]

Likewise, demystifying production techniques used to internalize the theological debate have the effect of placing Jesus outside history, dislocating him from the cultural and political forces of his time. In an inside-out world of Jesus' guilty conscience, all historical markers lose their mooring. His attempts to resolve spiritual and social conflicts around him are ineffective because the primary struggle between good and evil occurs within his conscience, not in the external world.

A contemporized Jesus has replaced the traditional externalized and mystified character by releasing him from his historical context. Timothy Corrigan provides a relevant frame of reference for understanding the effect of such a separation of narrative from historical context, "The character no longer brings the viewer back to the historical moment to recapture its essence. Instead, the perspective is that of a collapsing narrative into the subjectivity of the character" (Corrigan 162). No longer the victim of universal forms of evil derived from cosmic forces, Jesus becomes a victim of his own religious delusions. The sacrificial victim turns himself over to the "hound of heaven," not to save humanity, but to end his mental torment. The Christ character, as a sacrificial victim, is not persecuted primarily by outside forces; instead he is victimized by his own conscience.

The use of point-of-view camera in the film allows for a personalized, dynamic, and fluid transfer of Jesus' religious struggle from an externalized setting to the psychological context of the victim's mind. Production techniques embed profane thoughts and images in the protagonist's mind, casting doubt on the relevance of the symbol as a source of universal appeal.[12]

It is worth noting that traditional treatments such as *King of Kings, The Greatest Story Ever Told,* and *Jesus* place the viewer outside of Jesus' mind, thus insuring his theological stability and universal appeal. For example, Nicholas Ray's Christ speaks and acts in uniform theological statements. In George Stevens's *Greatest Story Ever Told,* Jesus gestures and theological meanings are communicated. Franco Zefferelli's *Jesus of Nazareth* contemporizes Christ's dialogue but maintains the same organizing qualities that render Jesus' consciousness inaccessible. In these films, Jesus' soul is revealed only partially through his onscreen behavior and expressions. They treat Jesus mind as a neutral area, a sacred space inaccessible to viewers, comprising a shared mystery. For the traditional Christ film, Jesus' mind represents the core of a stable religious system, the nonpartisan ground whereby viewers may fill in religious meanings, personalizing the intent of the sacrificial victim's redemptive act. This externalization of Christ's motivation insures the universality of the Christ character as a redemptive symbol. What Scorsese tears away from the classical Christ films through point-of-view and voiceover narration is precisely what is required to legitimize the traditional system of scapegoating, a mentally stable and morally resolute victim whose behavior reinforces clear boundaries between good and evil.

The film's victimization of traditional Christianity is made apparent when nonconforming images and ideas about Jesus are placed in viewers minds, thus erasing or displacing conventional associations and references. A good example of this process can be found in a brief, passing image of a woman drawing water from a well, calling up a familiar biblical association of the Samaritan woman found in the fourth chapter of the Gospel of John. In Scorsese's portrayal the woman is shown topless; she draws water in such a way so as to emphasize her chest area. Her shoulders are squared to the point-of-view camera shot for a full frontal view of her breasts. She seductively looks into Jesus' eyes (the camera) as he passes. The effect of such imagery is to saturate a familiar Bible story with erotic qualities violating sacred or holy references to the biblical character. The idea that a first-century Palestinian woman would appear topless in public is inaccurate and, quite frankly, absurd. Nevertheless, the scene gives the impression through point-of-view camera that Palestinian women did dress in this manner. It infers that not only *could* Jesus have looked at her in this way, he *did* look at her in precisely this way. The camera operates as a rhetorical tool, demystifying Christ's mind and implicating the viewer as the originating source of profanity and voyeurism.[13] Such images become implicated in the activity of scapegoating at the point of reception where offensive ideas are recognized and their meanings are publicly contested.

Scorsese and his supporters have responded to such interpretations by arguing that the image of a topless woman at a well has no rhetorical aim, it does nothing more than provide us with the possible mental struggle facing the reluctant messiah. Because the event is confined to his conscience, Jesus' effort to do the right thing, as he looks at the highly sexualized image of the woman is inconsequential. This strategic deflection of the image's offensive qualities relies on a privatized interpretation of its meaning, that the meaning of such images is a matter of private and personal taste rather than one derived from collective and public debate. According to this way of thinking, any argument that contests the scene's religious legitimacy must also provide evidence that the historical Jesus did not actually experience such thoughts. This defense relies on the lay person's naivete, lack of knowledge of the biblical story and an uncritical view of production methods. None of Scorsese's contemporaries would suggest that these images are neutral or accidental.[14] Directors craft point-of-view shots, intentionally shaping the viewer's experience and deliberately constructing them as cultural statements that should be respected and taken seriously.

DREAMING TEMPTATION

The film's most significant challenge to the traditional conservative Christian view comes in the dream sequence in which Jesus is tempted to come down off the cross and live a normal life. It provides important clues about the film's primary argument and its victimization of traditional Christianity. Widely recognized as the pinnacle of the film's blasphemous message, the dream sequences presents a complex and conflicted message concerning Jesus' resistance to temptation, his death, and resurrection. Acting as a subjunctive insertion the dream asks, "What if Jesus had chosen to live a normal human life?"

Scorsese has defended the film's presentation of the last temptation as an affirmation of Christ's free will choice to die on the cross. "In the film, the *last temptation* was to live the life of an ordinary man and die in old age" (Rensin 59). The content of the dream, however, contradicts this assertion in important ways. In it Jesus is unable to distinguish between God and the Devil and incapable of resisting the enticements presented to him in the fantasy. As a result, the dream operates not as affirmative evidence of Jesus' moral resolve but as a means of negating the Christian type of sacrificial victim and the claims associated with him.

A bit of background information will help set up the next portion of the analysis. Temptation plays an important role in the Christ story and formalizes the function of the scapegoat as a source of guilt reduction. Traditionally the temptation scene is meant to provide evidence that the sacrificial victim has free will to choose between two distinct moral outcomes. Jesus' denial of the Devil's offer insures his fate as a Christian victim worthy of his place as a holy savior and founder of the Christian religion. Temptation, as a biblical concept, assumes there is a risk involved in Jesus' free-will choice, the potential loss of the sacrificial victim's holiness and a threat to the biblical system that transfers guilt from humans to supernatural entities. Temptation has collective moral consequences for the Christian religion, in part because the sacrificial victim willingly chooses his fate. In more traditional presentations, Jesus' refusal to give in to the forces of evil legitimizes the Christian Church and its moral code. His triumph over temptation reifies the guilt of humanity (in the form of sin) and makes the death and resurrection events meaningful as forces of human renewal. His free-will choice to die on the cross a victim of human sin also produces a division between human and divine forms of motivation. The Christian system of scapegoating relies on the fixed polarity between narrative forces of good and evil. As a result of this polarity a holy sacrifice is produced. Resistance to temptation operates as the key element in confirming the victim's free will choice to follow a path of suffering and death, confirming the theological explanation for the atonement.

Temptation, as presented in the *Last Temptation,* produces a much different outcome primarily because the sacrificial victim's freedom is contrived. Jesus is never free of the internal torment that tempts him in various ways. Thus, when he resists temptation in the desert sequence, the achievement is of little consequence because his internal struggle has not been resolved. Without the resolution of this internal tension the sacrifice cannot stand for a free-will choice to die on the cross, and as a result, his death cannot come to represent the transfer of human sin onto a risen savior.

The film's content, particularly the dream sequence, confirms that Jesus falsely imagines he is free to choose an alternative life. At the outset of the dream Jesus is delirious, semiconscious, dying on the cross. He suddenly becomes aware that something is different about the situation. Silence demarcates the cinematic transition into his hallucination. Compelled by her beauty, Jesus believes the girl standing at the foot of the cross is an angel from God. She removes the spikes and helps him down. Jesus takes her hand and walks into the world he might have inhabited. The dust settles and the sun breaks through the clouds. Jesus looks up wondering if he is dead; he looks around and sees the crowd still carrying on behind a wall of silence. An angel stands at the foot of his cross. Jesus asks, "Who are you?" The Guardian Angel responds, "I'm your guardian angel . . . He doesn't want your blood. Come with me" The two pass through the crowd and Jesus asks, "You mean I'm not the messiah?" She responds, "No."

If we derive our interpretation from this material the dream sequence clearly testifies that Jesus accepts Satan's tempting offer. He is captivated by the girl-angel who effectively persuades him that he is not the messiah. Taking her hand, Jesus gladly follows her into his alternative future life failing to recognize the angel is Satan. He changes his mind only after having lived to an old age in the dream.

In the rather lengthy hallucination, we then follow Jesus, fast-forward, through 37 years of life as a normal person.[15] At the end of this dream life, as he lies dying, his disciples return to visit him and lament his choice to live as a man. When confronted by Judas at the very end of his fantasy life Jesus argues, "But my guardian angel . . . " Judas fires back, "Your guardian angel. Look at her! Satan. Shame on you traitor" (97). Realizing he mistook the Devil for an angel, Jesus relents, crawling back to the cross as he begs God to forgive him for the mistake and allow him to be the messiah. "Will you listen to a selfish, unfaithful son?" Recognizing he has been tricked, Jesus then changes his mind.

The sequence provides no evidence to suggest that Jesus resisted the Devil's temptation. He is easily persuaded to come off the cross to live the rest of his life as a person. As a result of this failure to resist, the crucifixion, as a freely chosen sacrificial act, is exposed as a fraud because Jesus fails to choose the moral path identified with the Christian salvation plan. His role as a type of Christian sacrificial victim is compromised and the moral outcome reversed—evil triumphs over good.[16]

One could argue that Jesus resists temptation based on the fact that he is not actually conscious when he accepts the angel's invitation to come down from the cross. This explanation is also unconvincing because it suggests that waking up from a dream constitutes an act of free will. Common sense tells us that under such contrived conditions, Jesus is neither conscious nor capable of acting on his decision to refuse Satan. The victim simply dreams he refuses temptation; he is bound, semiconscious, and nailed to a cross when he makes the choice.

SAVING JESUS FROM CHRISTIANITY

The dream-tation, a fiction within a fiction, creates an ideal context for showcasing the film's polemical view of Jesus and the conversation between Jesus and Paul at the market provides its most potent appeal. In this extraordinary encounter Jesus denies his own role in authoring Christianity, making his death and resurrection irrelevant and unnecessary. While it is presented as a hypothetical insertion, the scene produces the film's most effective reformulation of the sacrificial victim whereby Jesus becomes alienated from Christianity.

Dreaming his new life, Jesus travels with his family to the market where he meets Paul, a parody of the Christian televangelist. Schrader describes the character "standing straight, radiating confidence. He speaks with the evangelistic fervor of a born-again Christian" (Schrader 89). Harry Dean Stanton plays an insincere charismatic—reminiscent of many such characters of the 1980s—who pitches his new religion to those who will listen. When he finds out who Jesus is, Paul launches into his argument, "Look around you. Look at their suffering and un-happiness. Their only hope is a resurrected Jesus. I don't care if you are Jesus or not. The resurrected Jesus will save the world. That's all that matters." Here the relationship between the film's controversial message and its victimization of traditional Christianity is most transparent.

The diatribe continues as Paul directly challenges the historical valid-ity of the resurrection, insisting that the life, death, and resurrection of Jesus do not matter. "I don't care if you are Jesus or not. The resurrected Jesus will save the world, that's all that matters." Jesus responds to Paul asking, "The world can be saved by lies?" Paul retorts, "What's truth? I've created truth out of longing and faith. I don't struggle with truth, I build it." A clever fabrication of a Jewish televangelist, Jesus is stripped of his mystical characteristics.

The dream's anti-Christian invective peaks with Paul's assertion that Christ's death and resurrection are unimportant, "If its necessary to save the world to crucify you, then I will crucify you and I'll resurrect you, like it or not." Paul adopts language of persecutor as he upbraids and belittles the savior turned family man. His statements tear away the re-ligious system of Christian faith breaking the last thread connecting the sacrificial victim to his Christian roots. The sacrality and holiness of Christ are completely expunged from the narrative, leaving a whimper-ing, weak Jesus who has nothing in common with the Christian savior. In a brilliant rhetorical move, the film turns the Christian message on its head. Jesus bequeaths his religious authority to Paul by denying he died on the cross, "I was never crucified on the cross, I'm alive." (91). By refuting the historical validity of the religion he authors the sacrificial victim is estranged from his traditional function as the Christian scapegoat.

The content of the dream does not support an interpretation that Jesus resisted temptation. At most, it confirms that Jesus hallucinated a se-quence of ideas about a hypothetical life that would further invalidate his religious mission and dilute his role as an innocent victim. Guilty of having failed to resist—while bound and dreaming—the Jesus figure becomes saturated with the characteristics of a profane and guilty victim, one quite different from those produced in the traditional Christ film. Near the end of the dream, he regrets having thought of himself as the messiah, "I am so ashamed of all the wrong ways I looked for God" (92). The film cleverly projects Jesus' failure to exercise free will onto the source of torment, a God most clearly identified with the Christian religion and the source blamed for his bondage and death. Shrouded in this mask of imagined free will the victim becomes Christianity itself.

In contrast to the *Last Temptation*'s secularized sacrificial victim, the victim found in traditional Christ films portrays his resistance to temptation as a ritualized act of free will. The free will and moral sanctity of the sacrificial victim are intact and uncompromised through ritualized exercise of choice, which produces a predetermined outcome. He collaborates with the divine source of persecution in his crucifixion. He hands himself over to the Christian God and thus becomes a supernatural religious figure through the resurrection. In the *Last Temptation,* however, Jesus does not collaborate with God in the same way. His death fails to represent a symbolic merging with God because his resistance to temptation does not constitute an act of free will required of such a synthesis.

In spite of these incongruities, it matters very little whether or not Jesus actually resists temptation because the function of temptation in the *Last Temptation* is not linked to its traditional antecedents. Its function here is to break down the social hierarchy of the Christian religion and reduce religion to a private personal experience. "It takes you to the point where there are no churches, just you alone with God" (Scorsese 27).

WAKING UP DEAD

When Jesus regains consciousness, and realizes he is actually dying on the cross, he says, "It is accomplished." Church bells ring as the film reel runs out in anticipation of the resurrection. Scorsese says the film's ending anticipates this event affirming the traditional view that Christ rose from the grave. "He transcends: He goes to heaven. What more could you want from life than salvation?" (Hodenfeld 38). But Scorsese's feelings about the seminal event in Christian history are likewise ambiguous. "I believe it happened. I do have doubts" (Kelly 243). He isn't sure about the relevance of the resurrection. "I can't say exactly what the resurrection means" (243). These directorial ambiguities are embedded in the film's ending, which lacks the essential ingredient for producing a legitimate Christian scapegoat.[17] Scorsese argues these factors do not invalidate his Christ from being the Christian savior, "He had to die to give us hope" (Kelly 243). His repeated claim that Jesus fulfilled the expectations of the Christian scapegoat indicate that, at the least, Scorsese failed to recognize the importance of the resurrection for producing a legitimate sacrificial victim in the Christian tradition. The director and screenwriter claim that their religious motives were genuine and their film produced a legitimate sacrificial victim. What they fail to do is admit the function of such alterations in producing a competing religious claim about Jesus' religious identity. The dialectic between film content and these authorial comments must be read as a play of blame, as the film's meanings, when taken literally, do not match the interpretation provided by the director.

The most reasonable explanation for the film's omission of the resurrection is that its inclusion would contradict the film's ambiguous view of Jesus' divine nature. This absence, as W. Barnes Tatum points out, helps sustain a view that the resurrection was a hoax (166). Adding the resurrection would reverse the film's privatized view of deity and the religious experience producing unequivocal representations of good and evil and contradict the moral relativism, which dominates the film narrative.

DISCLAIMING CULPABILITY

As we have seen, the dream's significance as a rhetorical device is established through its contradictory messages about temptation produced in the dream sequence. It is described by the director as a traditional temptation event, when in fact there is no evidence in the film to support the claim. When faced with such contradictions, the director has often adopted a contrary position, arguing that the film is a fictional presentation that makes no claims about the New Testament Christ figure. The disclaimer at the beginning of the film provides the most prominent evidence of this rhetorical strategy. "This film is not based upon the Gospels but upon the fictional exploration of the eternal spiritual conflict." When asked about the film's subject matter, Scorsese contradicts himself and the film's disclaimer with statements that confirm his intention to produce a serious biblical film, "I've always wanted to do a film about the life of Christ" (Scorsese, *Scorsese On* 116).

Strategically placed at the front of the film, the disclaimer asks viewers to consider the film's religious story seriously but ignore its religious context, Christian scriptures. In an important and necessary separation of entertainment film from religious experience, the disclosure counts on an assumption that movies are privatized fictional worlds of escapist entertainment, creative and original works of art that appeal only privately to aesthetic taste. The disclaimer and its underlying assumption, engage an activity of blame in the form of denial, setting up the film's radical interpretation of the Christ story.

When taken at face value, the disclaimer is unconvincing. It is quite clear that the film and the book that preceded it are based on the Gospels of the New Testament. Kazantzakis did not conjure up the names Jesus, Judas, or Mary Magdalene. Nor was the book's historical context, first century Palestine, arbitrarily chosen by the Greek author. His characters and story come from the New Testament Gospels. To adopt the New Testament story, its characters, plot elements, historical context, religious themes, while arguing that the film is "not based on the Gospels" is, on its face, ludicrous and hypocritical. It is tactical, part of the film's rhetorical purpose, the repudiation of the traditional filmic treatment of the Christ story and the Christian Church. Through the disclaimer the film and its creators assert their right to freely interpret historical events while denying accountability for such interpretations.

The film retains its rhetorical coherence for audiences by maintaining this textual ambiguity through the lack of understanding on the part of the public concerning the process of filmmaking and meanings found in the New Testament. The fact that so little has been made of these observations concerning the film's disclaimer testifies to the film's effectiveness as a rhetorical document.

CONCLUDING REMARKS

Martin Scorsese wanted to make a film about the life of Jesus, one that would strip the story of all its traditional elements. In the process he made a film that thoroughly demystified the Christ character, detaching him from those patterns traditionally associated with the Christ film and its biblical antecedents. In his attempt to give the story new meaning and relevance Scorsese psychologized and subjectivized the story, turning it into a struggle for inner peace. Believing that original art provokes and challenges Scorsese stripped key elements held sacred to conservative Christians in the name of original art and freedom of speech. The film rejects its traditional religious roots for a secularized religious sensibility. As a result, Scorsese's Jesus is an embodiment of the postmodern culture; he distrusts Christian religious institutions and their doctrine.

He views his own religious experience with suspicion and his religious inclinations never gain dominance over his doubts because religion, being unenlightened and irrational, contradicts his secularized sensibilities.

In the *Last Temptation,* Jesus is transformed into a multivocal, heterogeneous and politically correct type of 1980s liberal America. This freethinking, pluralistic man qualifies as an appropriate victim for removal of their collective guilt. Along his path of liberation he rejects the religious absolutes of Christianity and the limits of its moral code. He fulfills his religious mission by cleansing himself of the superstitions of his filmic predecessors and the religion they represent. Jesus' victimization on the cross produces a form of redemption, not the form identified with traditional Christianity, but a secular redemption of the autonomous conscience conformed to the principles of humanism. The Christian story is replaced with a myth of progress, "the myth that humanity will gradually become liberated and divine through its own instrumentality" (Eliade 203). This redemption is achieved by sacrificing traditional religious beliefs in the form of an appropriate victim, one who embodies all of the traits and characteristics of the system of belief itself. Through the sacrifice of a conflicted and unholy messiah, the film jettisons all of the traditional baggage identifying Jesus with traditional Christianity.

NOTES

1. According to the biographer and translator P. A. Bien, Kazantzakis was a spiritual pilgrim all his life and he traveled extensively around Europe, the Middle East, and China (499). During his adult life he was a prolific writer and *The Last Temptation of Christ* was his final work (finished in 1955).

2. The church is referred to in terms of a uniform acceptance of Jesus as the atoning sacrifice for human sin and his role as a divine figure.

3. When released in the late 1950s, the book caused nationwide protests in Greece and much of the surrounding area.

4. These observations provide important background information for this examination of the film telling us how the Christ story was conceptualized and brought to the screen. God is the primary persecutorial force behind Jesus' suffering and death. While all Christ films place God in the role of persecutor, in that Jesus is predestined to die according to God's plan. In traditional Christ films Jesus embraces his role as God's collaborator. In *The Last Temptation,* God is an adversarial force that Jesus actively resists. As we shall see later in this analysis, these changes have an important impact on the function of the sacrificial victim in a religious ritual of scapegoating.

5. His biographers have examined Scorsese's motives and have quoted him extensively on the subject. They, for the most part, take his statements of Chris-

tian commitment at face value. For these writers, Scorsese's religious beliefs are not a matter for debate but of individual reflection and conviction. In their analyses, his personal religious motives are left largely unexamined. Among the authors referred to are Les Keyser, Mary Pat Kelly, David Ehrenstein, Michael Bliss, and Marie Katheryn Connelly.

6. Scorsese's collaborator on *Taxi Driver,* Schrader agreed to write the screenplay and distilled the 500-page book into the 35 scenes he felt were most significant. Schrader organized the script around a key question, "What does God want of me?; or how they related to the central triangle of the film, which is Jesus, Judas and Magdalene" (Schrader, *On Schrader* 135).

7. The Christ film refers to dramatic presentations of the life of Christ. The genre excludes comedic (*Life of Brian*), allegorical (*Jesus of Montreal*), and musical (*Jesus Christ Superstar*) representations.

8. Icons always present their subject as vital, dynamic, and living mysteries that audiences encounter in order to convey religious insight. This iconographic representation of Jesus requires a fixed and stable consciousness (Eliade 21). This fixed center is at once both historical and contextual, a Jesus of the Bible and a Jesus of the film's period. Jeffrey Hunter reflects the cultural trappings of the 1960s while communicating eternal truths about God.

9. Both the form and content of Ray's *King of Kings* present the sacred as otherworldly. This Jesus is divested, for the most part, of the trappings of human struggle, thus the film operates as the metaphoric equivalent of the status quo relations between Hollywood and the Christian religion. It serves as an official representation of a stable power structure in which social allegiances are incorporated into a national ethos. The *Last Temptation* collapses the mystical elements of the Christ character and thus also reflects a collapse of the boundaries that have long distinguished Hollywood from its religious counterpart.

10. W. Barnes Tatum makes this observation on page 169 of his examination of the film.

11. Bruce Babbington observes this Jesus in mentally unstable. "The *Last Temptation* presents a fragmented, almost schizophrenic Jesus. Even the signs of his possession by God are ambiguous, something like epilepsy, that could be madness or repressed sexual desire" (Babbington 152).

12. Point-of-view camera technique is not in itself damning; what the camera sees as Jesus' eyes, however, is quite significant for the film's formation of cultural victims. The diagesis produces a cinematic space in which profane imagery comes to permeate and dominate the plot.

13. One of the more striking things about this image is how it strips the woman of her subjectivity and humanity, making her the pure object of the male gaze.

14. Scorsese's authorial claims of religious sincerity can easily disguise cinematic provocation because film technology has no uniform and coherent theological signage. This analysis takes the debate over the Christ film, another step toward producing such signage.

15. Jesus marries Magdalene, and goes to work as a carpenter. God visits Magdalene in her late pregnancy and gently kills her. Jesus, distraught over the turn of events, continues his domestic life, taking Martha and her sister Mary as wives. At one point in the dream Jesus, his wives, and children travel to the market where Jesus overhears Paul, a parodic figure of televangelistic proportion, preaching about a man who died for their sins.

16. Strangely enough, out of the thousands of pages written about the film and dream sequence, in the years since the film's release very little has been said about these contradictions.

17. Numerous explanations have been provided for its absence. One view argues that viewers understand and assume the resurrection occurs, thus it isn't necessary to include it in the film. Another rationalization asserts that, because the resurrection is not in the book, it should not be in the film. Finally, it can be argued that adding the resurrection would have lengthened the already long two-hour and 20-minute film. Although these arguments are helpful in explaining the absence of the resurrection, none of them is particularly convincing.

Chapter 4

COUNTERING BLASPHEMY

The *Last Temptation* conflict developed as a process whereby pressures and tensions between two emerging positions became better defined. At some point in the conflict the demand for retribution produced a particular type of ritual of blame whereby one social segment took specific aim at the other and launched into retribution—acts of antagonism and rhetorical scapegoating. The two primary segments involved in this victimization can be distinguished by the peculiarities of their rhetorical positions and how they protected privileged ideas about sacred matters—those things held most dear. This chapter explores the two positions, religious conservative and liberal progressive, and examines the language they employed to bring transgressive ideas back into arrangements of the broader society. Of particular interest are the negative forms of religious rhetoric, adopted by both main voices, and the role of sociopolitical hierarchy in which agents were formed and acted, and against which they reacted (Burke, *Rhetoric of Religion* 187).[1]

Scapegoating is a process set in action when the ordinary lines of reasoning, social protocol, and other language of conciliation are exhausted. In the *Last Temptation* controversy, this breakdown occurs gradually as parties fail to provide one another satisfactory explanations. As a result of this breakdown there is a collapse of the debate into a rudimentary language of blame that posits roles of victim and victimizer according to distinct separation of what is considered good and evil. The boundaries between these perspectives are not always well defined and in the exchange of accusations it is often unclear just who is victimizing whom. Initially, religious conservatives portrayed themselves as victims of blasphemy, while late in the conflict the role shifts to some degree when liberal progressives argue they were being persecuted as victims of censorship.

Religious conservatives were alarmed that a Hollywood studio would support the making of a film that contradicted their dearest values. The threat, in their view, was to the cohesion of the religious conservative sense of religious identity. Their public response to the film was a vociferous attempt to reestablish the sacred stature of their savior, and to strengthen long-held boundaries between secular and religious domains. The liberal progressive community, for the most part, disregarded and discredited these religious concerns and sought to extend the boundaries of artistic expression.

In this exchange, social ills are purged in a process of catharsis and cleansing. The early developments of linguistic scapegoating are highlighted for examination, and for studying the points of juncture between social segments at their moment of breakdown (Burke, *Grammar of Motives* 406).

The dissociation and alienation produced by scapegoating develops from distinct structures of power, social hierarchies that sustain and reinforce themselves in periodic encounters with competing worldviews. These hierarchies are constructed around rules and laws that cannot be fully kept; thus there is guilt production, which, in turn, produces rituals of purgation and cleansing (400). Once the guilt is purged the social order returns to a state of equilibrium.

Scapegoating, as a guilt-releasing mechanism, allowed each position in the *Last Temptation* controversy a release from culpability and blame by transferring guilt to the appropriate victim. The developments of the process mapped out here are viewed as historically situated in a three-phase process. Initially the two segments share identities within the larger social configuration whereby a common language links the two as part of the larger cultural entity. At some point in the correspondence and communication, this common linguistic link is broken and the individual segments begin to engage in a rhetorical process of segregation whereby the distinctive qualities of the subgroups are emphasized as a means of ritually alienating the offending party (*Grammar* 407).

In the *Last Temptation* controversy, alliances were formed around sacred beliefs and life stances demarcated here in terms of liberal progressive and religious conservative. This chapter primarily analyzes the religious conservative position on the *Last Temptation* in the context of verbal and written exchanges, which advance the process of ritualized blame. It studies how religious conservatives viewed the film, its offensive content, and the rhetorical strategies applied to reestablish order.

The stages of scapegoating, as they occurred in the *Last Temptation* controversy, are examined first in the early correspondence between Universal Studios and key religious conservative leaders. It examines several texts to better understand how the relations between the two views became so conflicted and antagonistic. These texts demonstrate certain aspects of the scapegoating process and the distinctive formulation of its victims. The complaint letter from an Idaho resident and first Universal letter, for example, characterize the initial conditions of dialogue and negotiation whereby there is a language of shared boundaries over the symbol Jesus (Poland 214). The second set of letters, those of Bill Bright, Universal's response (to him), and Jack Valenti's press statement, are examined for ways they introduce a rhetorical challenge to these common boundaries in a language of scapegoating (Harmetz, "Top Studios Support" C18).

The examination of the early correspondence between Universal and key religious leaders provides a foundation for the following chapters' presentation of a body of textual material that further demonstrates how scapegoating occurred. Chapter 5 applies the same analytic structure to the liberal progressive backlash and studies a range of views and statements presented from this view. Chapter 6 shifts the focus to a television text, the *Oprah Winfrey* program, to examine how scapegoating occurs in such a public forum. The final segment, Chapter 7, analyzes scapegoating and legal discourse. Combined, these chapters are representative of the stages of scapegoating, from a merger in shared boundaries, to a condition of ritualized alienation, and, finally, to a new position of merger in the dialectical opposition to the other.

INITIATING BLAME

The tensions between these two sides were, initially, not very prominent or distinctive. The early developments that took place months before the film's release consisted mainly of the negotiations between Universal and a small group of religious conservatives. Although it was considered a threat, the film was far from release and religious leaders felt there was hope that Universal would respond to their concerns. Early correspondence is punctuated with this hopefulness. Still, in it one sees conservative anxiety beginning to take shape and form. This material does not have highly charged language and does not openly challenge Universal.

It maintains a linguistic formality that demonstrates a shared responsibility. There is shared space in the language that allows for options based on continued communication.

The initial stage of scapegoating in this ongoing communication is marked by an issue, a condition of transgression, or a felt sense of violation on the part of religious conservatives. The severity of this violation is measured by the strength of the reaction and by how religious conservatives responded to the studio's resistance to their demands.

Attempts were made through a variety of communication media to convince Universal not to go through with the production and to halt the planned release of the film. Mr. and Mrs. C.R. of Pocatello, Idaho, sent one such appeal in a letter, in February 1988. We find in this letter a shared sense of responsibility for the controversy over the film:

> Universal Studios
> Louis Wasserman
> This is a letter to inform you that I ask you not to release the movie "The Last Temptation of Christ." Our family and others will not watch it (and get others to do the same). You are putting a bad name on yourself if you let the movie be released.
> The subject matter of the movie personally bothers me. It contradicts everything the Bible teaches. We ask you not to release this movie.
> Thank you,
> Mr. and Mrs. C.R. (qtd. in Poland 212)

Even though the C.R. family was against Universal's release of the film, they approached the studio head with a degree of civility conveyed through the letter's courteous tone and apparent sincerity. The unsophisticated language is emotional, communicating personal feelings and concerns. An option for reconciliation remains open, and the writer hesitates to move beyond a certain courtesy in the expectation that the hoped-for response will occur.

Universal received tens of thousands of such letters and responded by defending the film's message and its director in words calling for moderation. The film studio found itself in the strange position of defending the film's religious message based on the personal convictions of its director.

The following letter from Universal to Campus Crusade for Christ is a general response to conservative concerns such as those expressed in C.R.'s letter. In it Universal demonstrates an awareness of conservative audience sensitivities and there is an attempt to quell rumors about the film:

Mar. 4, 1988
   Dear Mr. Beehler,
   We, at Universal Pictures, appreciate your letter of inquiry about "The Last Temptation of Christ." We understand that there are many untrue rumors circulating about the movie. Since you have taken the time to write us, we would like to share with you the thoughts and desires of the director about his motion picture.
   "The Last Temptation of Christ" is a motion picture that I have wanted to make for over fifteen years. Both as a filmmaker and a Christian, I believe with all my heart that the film I am making is a deeply religious one. Although Jesus is tempted by Satan, what the movie says and what I believe is that Jesus resisted temptation and was crucified as told in the Bible. I have made a film, which is an affirmation of faith, and I urge everyone not to judge my film until they see it.
   With great sincerity,
   Martin Scorsese

   As reported in the news section of the March 4, 1988, edition of Christianity Today, our Christian consultant, Tim Penland, in association with Universal Pictures, will hold advance screenings of the film for a select group of evangelical leaders far in advance of the release of the picture.
   We appeal to your sense of fairness in this matter and it is our hope that you will delay judgment until you see the film.
   Sincerely,
   Roger Armstrong (studio pr)
   Universal Studios (qtd. in Poland 38)

In a symbolic defense of "fairness," Armstrong asks concerned Christians to exercise restraint and calls on conservatives to defer judgment until they have at least seen the film. Confident that the movie is what Scorsese says it is, an "affirmation of faith," the studio endorses his explanation. "What the movie says and what I believe is that Jesus resisted temptation and was crucified as told in the Bible." The letter claims that there is no offensive content in the film and implies that the negative reaction by some conservatives is due to a misunderstanding of the movie and its director.

Scorsese's personal testimony provides a shared element, and the religious subject matter provides a linguistic bridge between the two worlds. In line with this reasoning, the letter endorses Scorsese's religious position and defends the film's unique religious message as something that is shared. The letter's appeal to religious conservative sense of fairness is thus a call for religious tolerance.

Scorsese's religious sincerity, however, could not sustain the Rev. Bright's confidence, especially as other developments had influenced his posture toward the studio. One of those developments involved the surfacing of a pirated screenplay; the other had to do with the studio's failure to send a representative to a meeting held by the Rev. Bright. The tone for future interaction would be more strained since religious conservatives gradually lost confidence in the studio's sincerity.

The cadre of religious leaders negotiating with Universal began to change their strategy as communication broke down in spring of 1988. The Rev. Bright, Larry Poland, and Tim Penland stopped looking for reconciliation and at some point began to focus solely on strategies to thwart Universal's plans to release the film. In a brainstorming session Bright came up with a possible solution to the problem: buy the film. But the studio head, Lew Wasserman, showed no interest in the offer. Bright's proposal is presented in the following letter to Wasserman and Universal. His suggestion that Universal sell him the film marks an important development in the scapegoat process and in the escalation of the conflict. It is a gesture of reconciliation whereby religious conservatives could reestablish their control of the dominant symbol, Jesus, and realign the boundaries between religious and secular realms:

July 1988

Dear Mr. Wasserman:

I am sorry that you were unavailable for a private meeting with our group. We wanted to discuss a proposal with you whereby I would personally be responsible for reimbursing Universal Pictures for the amount already invested in the movie The Last Temptation of Christ. In exchange, you would provide me with all of the copies of the film (which would be promptly destroyed) and its distribution rights. I anticipate that the money will be provided by concerned individuals across America who will pool their resources in order to cover your costs.

Although I do not represent any particular religious group or denomination in this matter, I stand in the tradition of classical

Christianity, which embraces all the major branches of Christendom.

I would like to discuss this proposal with you in the same spirit in which Pope John Paul II told the media in Los Angeles last September, "The church stands ready to help you by her encouragement and to support you in all your worthy aims."

The letter quoted extensively from Pope John Paul's appeal to the media community to exercise its influence responsibly and concluded: "The central message of the Christian faith is that Jesus Christ paid for our sins on the cross, and that by accepting His gift of salvation we are able to choose eternal life over death. It is in the spirit of the Savior of all men who paid for my mistakes that I am prepared to help you in this way."

Please contact my office by July 19 with your response.

Sincerely,

Bill Bright

cc: Pat Broeske/John Dart, the Los Angeles Times (Poland 123)

The emotional force of this letter derives from deep feelings of ownership of the dominant symbol Jesus. Likewise, the moral function of the purchase proposal is clear: to protect the symbol from corrupting images and ideas. It is also clear from the content of the letter itself that Bright felt a courtesy had been violated by Universal's failure to attend the meeting. It is unclear as to the value or significance of the meeting about which Bright speaks. What seems very clear is that Universal defended its intentions as being honorable. Nevertheless, the shift in religious conservative strategy had already occurred. For Bright, Universal's failure to attend the meeting presented an opportunity for a more pronounced display of power to establish control of the high moral ground. Whether or not the lack of attendance was an act of defiance is of little significance. What is worth noting is how the letter signals a change in the religious conservative strategy. The tone of the letter is combative and confrontational, a challenge to Wasserman and Universal. It subsumes all secular mandates within the religious order by exerting moral authority over the content of a popular film.

The language of scapegoat is enlisted to reestablish hierarchical relations between secular and religious domains. This is achieved, in part, by placing Universal in a submissive role evident in Bright's reference to the authority of classical Christianity and his use of the quote from the pope that, in tandem, sets up the hierarchy to whom all should obey and respond. His desire to help Universal in "its worthy aims" is a subtle attempt to subordinate the studio to God and his primary representative, Bill Bright, who personifies his authority in God.

The purchase offer had currency with religious conservatives including Rev. Larry Poland. Rev. Poland's reflection on the offer reveals the rhetorical undertow of the group's religious motivation. "We would own it. We could do what we wanted. We would probably have a public celebration and burn it. I loved the idea because, for my money, it created a classic dilemma for Universal, a lose/lose situation" (117). For Rev. Poland and Bright the best solution would be one where they had ownership of the transgressive object. Poland imagines "burning" the film in a joyous ritual of purgation, the ultimate enactment of restoration of the social hierarchy and the affirmation of conservative doctrine. In actuality, there was no solid financial support for the idea. It was a bluff (Poland 122).

The Bright correspondence also demonstrates how the range of options for dialogue with Universal concerning the *Last Temptation* became more adversarial. In his letter one sees the diminishing reliance upon a language of reconciliation and openness. The tone of courtesy and mutual respect is abandoned for a more unified language of blame.

Universal had little to gain from selling the film and did not take the offer seriously. Instead, the studio took advantage of the situation, using it launch a publicity campaign to refute religious conservatives. Its refusal to sell might alienate some audiences, but a strong rebuttal would elevate the studio's status among its peers in the film community and reinforce a strong common bond with those who supported constitutional guarantees of free speech.

Exploiting the issue for its own gain, the studio presented its refusal letter to Bright in full-page newspaper ads (in both the *Los Angeles Times* and the *New York Times*). The message is a firm refusal based on principles of freedom, demonstrating transition in the studio's rhetoric toward a more pronounced language of scapegoating.

July 14, 1998

Dear Mr. Bright:

We at Universal Pictures have received your proposal in which you have offered to buy The Last Temptation of Christ which you would then destroy so that no one could ever see it. While we understand the deep feelings and convictions, which have prompted this offer, we believe that to accept it would threaten the fundamental freedoms of religion and expression promised to all Americans under our Constitution.

You have quoted Pope John Paul II on the film industry's "accountability to God, to the community and before the witness of history." Those who wrote the Constitution believed that all of these were best served by protecting freedom of speech, freedom of press, and freedom of religion. As Thomas Jefferson noted, 'Torrents of blood have been spilt in the Old World in consequence of vain attempts . . . to extinguish religious opinion.' The Twentieth Century has provided us with further evidence of the abuses, which occur when monolithic authorities regulate artistic expression and religious beliefs. Though those in power may justify the burning of books at the time, the witness of history teaches the importance of standing up for freedom of conscience even when the view being expressed may be unpopular.

You have expressed a concern that the content of the films be 'true.' But whose truth? If everyone in America agreed on all religious, political and artistic truths, there would be no need for our constitutional guarantees. Only in totalitarian states are all people forced to accept one version of truth. In any case, Martin Scorsese has stated clearly that his film is a work of fiction and that it is based on a novel, not the Gospels. It makes no claim whatsoever to be any more than a reflection of his own personal exploration.

In your letter you state that your position 'embraces all the major branches of Christendom.' But there always have been and continue to be many viewpoints among Christians. Many religious leaders of different denominations who attended our July 12 screenings in New York, which you declined to attend, were not offended by the film and even felt that it could be a tool for fruitful discussion. The Constitutional guarantee of freedom of religious expression was provided precisely to protect such diversity of opinions, including the highly personal views of Nikos Kazantzakis, Martin Scorsese, the film's writers and artists.

In the United States, no one sect or coalition has the power to set boundaries around each person's freedom to explore religious and philosophical questions whether through speech, books or films.

These freedoms protect us all.

They are precious.

They are not for sale.

Universal Pictures (quoted in Poland 124–26)

The letter calls up the patriotic ideals outlined in the Constitution. It reasons that selling the film to Bright would mean bowing to the "monolithic forces" in society and opening the door to new threats of censorship. Challenging this censorship, Universal declares that viewers should have a right to develop their own religious interpretations. In this regard, Universal and Scorsese are presented as defenders of the helpless, those who cannot fight the "monolithic forces" or "totalitarian" regimes alone. Likewise, the studio wraps itself in the tradition of Thomas Jefferson and the Founding Fathers. Thus, it may claim greater authority staking out the high moral ground.

Although the letter refrains from moving any further in its use of specific religious language, it does not hesitate to link those religious ideas of Martin Scorsese and Nikos Kazantzakis to the mandates given by Thomas Jefferson in the assertion that religious opinion should not be extinguished. There is both an adherence to, and denial of, religious beliefs. On the one hand, Universal denies the film's significance to Christianity, referring to the Christianity of the religious conservative. On the other hand, Universal defends the film as an artistic representation, a unique religious expression of its director with which it agrees: "It would threaten the fundamental freedoms of religion and expression promised to all Americans" (124). Religious ideas are adopted as a levering device for displacing religious conservative authority on such matters of popular films.

Naturally, the Universal strategy cannot be defined by this distinction alone—its use of religious language. Many other contributing factors contribute to the polemical content. In any event, Universal's use of religious language is of paramount importance for identifying the crossover from one language to the other in the process of scapegoating. Such language provides clues as to how the ritual object of blame is formulated, articulated, and presented by the studio. But, more important, it demonstrates a breaking down of the discourse as it begins to adopt the language and religious orientation of the opposition.

The strategies discussed here were implemented, in part because there was pressure on Universal to save face and distinguish their high aims from those of the lowly religious fanatics who threatened social stability and freedoms of speech. The studio was under considerable pressure from its constituencies to stand firmly upon the foundational mandates of the Constitution and the First Amendment. The Constitution is used to justify the strategies of alienation and to distinguish right and wrong, good and bad in terms of free speech.

In this respect the letter borrows from feelings of guilt everyone has about a democratic society—that it is not really pluralistic or fair but is instead a form of selective repression. This is the paradox of free speech advocacy—it must call for the inclusion of all points of view, on constitutional grounds, yet it must ritually remove those voices within its domain that fail to be inclusive (Fish 142). The object of blame—religious conservatism—allows Universal to maintain its location in the social hierarchy within which the democratic hierarchy continues to reside.

In part, these purposes are achieved by Universal through what Burke calls "tragic imitation" (Reuckert, *Kenneth Burke* 223). Although he is referring specifically to dramatism in poetry such as Shakespeare, one may make a correlation between this concept and the letter's imitation of the demonic and the rhetoric of scapegoating. In the scapegoat process the rhetoric often resorts to stylized imitation of the demonic as an object of projected guilt, and as the symbolic reworking of hierarchical uncertainty facing a democratic society. When guilt is projected as a means of releasing a party from accountability, it is no longer produced as a discourse unique to the segment itself; instead, the language bears the markings of a highly emotional reaction whereby the party involved resorts to stylized language of blame. Universal is able to both express and redeem the civic motive—freedom of speech—through the use of religious principles (223).

As the exchange between Universal and religious conservatives heated up, other players became interested in freedom of speech issues. Prominent leaders in Hollywood were compelled by Universal's argument. They converged on the issue, joining forces with the embattled studio in a defense of free expression and Constitutional guarantees. Jack Valenti, president of the Motion Picture Academy Association, issued a statement in support of Universal and booked visits on television talk shows to express his (and the industry's) views on the matter. Valenti's brief press statement reflects the general mood among many in Hollywood concerning the purchase offer and other strategies forwarded by religious conservatives (Harmetz, "Top Studios" C18). Importantly, the release carries the weighty endorsement of the major Hollywood studios: Columbia Pictures, the Walt Disney Company, MGM/UA Communications, Orion Pictures, Paramount Pictures, 20th Century Fox, and Warner Brothers.

In the release, Valenti challenges the religious conservative positions, insisting that the religious community's attempt to keep the film out of theaters is a violation of free expression (C18). His language solidifies the moral status of Universal and projects blame onto religious conservatives: "The key issue, the only issue, is whether or not self-appointed groups can prevent a film from being exhibited to the public, or a book from being published, or a piece of art from being shown. . . . The major companies of MPAA support MCA/Universal in its absolute right to offer to the people whatever movie it chooses" (C18). Valenti's point is simple, direct, and confrontational. He and the community he represents stand behind Universal in a unified adherence to Constitutional guarantees of free speech. In the language of absolutes Valenti argues that any restrictions on Universal's activity of filmmaking and distribution would involve an act of true evil, censorship. The movie, which is what religious conservatives have given much attention to, is not a matter for debate for Valenti. He sees such an interest as insignificant, and, instead of focusing on the films controversial message, argues for the protection of the studio's right to produce religious films.

CONFRONTING THE ENEMY

These letters provide some insight into the process by which a scapegoating language is developed and how the general tone of conciliation and negotiation shifts to language of confrontation, polarity and ritual alienation. Mr. and Mrs. C.R.'s letter is a plea, arguing for a certain response while withholding judgment. Universal's generic response to Bright and others is, likewise, a rational plea for calm that allows religious conservatives a role in the decision. Bright's letter carries a more combative language, as does the Universal response. Valenti's statement applies the rhetoric of raw power, that is, his ability to act on his belief in defiance of those who oppose him and the industry he defends. As the language becomes more based on opposites, stereotypes, and dramatic imitation, the distinctions between rhetorical positions tend to lose their distinctive characteristics and begin to look and sound like the other.

These texts indicate that important changes took place over a period of several months when Universal Studios was corresponding with concerned religious leaders. The correspondence studied here highlights those changes by way of the scapegoat motif. It appears to be a valid observation that both religious conservatives, and Universal and its supporters changed their posture toward one another in June and July 1988. For religious conservatives the threat involved the loss of ownership and control over their most sacred figure. For Universal the threat involved a perceived loss of control over the arena of popular film and the domain of free speech. These perceived threats to underlying assumptions about sacred matters motivated escalation in the conflict.

Evidence provided in these letters supports the finding that by early summer 1988 the two dominant oppositions had refined their accusations, in a logic of blame, and were producing more calcified rhetoric of the scapegoat. This hardened rhetoric has particular characteristics. It is to this area of analysis that this study now turns—to the religious conservative position and their accusations of blasphemy.

History demonstrates that religious conservatives have always maintained strong separation from the world of entertainment and Hollywood. From its very inception film has been scrutinized by religious groups and organizations for its corrupting influence on society (Moley 25). The mildly adversarial relationship was maintained in many respects because Hollywood has largely avoided religious subjects.[2] The discourse of popular film stayed away from that of the religious Christian. One could say that the two arenas spoke different languages that rarely overlapped.

What separates *Last Temptation* and the controversy surrounding it is the way a popular film became a focus for a broad cultural debate over religious beliefs, ideas, and values. In this sense, the film ritually transfers religious ideas of a previously separate discourse to the environment of popular film. Because of this overlap, religious conservatives became concerned that a popular film might portray their savior in unacceptable ways and that they might lose control over its use. In accordance with these observations is the recognition that scapegoating is inherently defensive; it rises out of felt threats to a community's identity and survival. For religious conservatives, the *Last Temptation* represented a potential loss of position within the social hierarchy, and more important, a loss of the power to control how society appropriates meaning to the Jesus figure.

Early in the conflict conservatives tried to get Universal to consider making major changes in the film, hoping they would take it off the market. These religious conservatives were opposed to the particular form of free speech presented in the *Last Temptation*. They saw the film more as a matter of a filmmaker using free speech to blaspheme the most holy figure in their religion. Thus their arguments often revolved around limiting a certain kind of speech—what could be said about Jesus.

The public nature of the debate coupled with the controversial nature of the film triggered strong emotional responses from religious conservatives. An outcry came, first from insiders such as Rev. Bill Bright and Tim Penland, and later from large numbers of Christian organizations and persuasions. Organizations such as AFA, Campus Crusade, 700 Club, Rosaries for Peace, Morality in Media, and local church and lay leaders became involved. Rumors about the film's blasphemous content were spread by media sources such as *Christianity Today,* Ted Baehr's *MOVIEGUIDE,* Billy Graham Ministries, James Dobson's *Focus on the Family,* Trinity Broadcasting, Rev. Jerry Falwell's *Old Time Gospel Hour,* Family Radio, Mother Angelica's ETWN, and scores of other radio and television outlets. Their response was a unified indignation developed from clearly focused perceptions about the film's offensive content.

The literature produced by these various religious organizations commonly carries a tone of embarrassment and humiliation. In a predominantly defensive and reactionary language, religious conservatives called out to the world, asking for understanding and recompense. When these appeals failed, a more emphatic language of blame was incorporated.

Religious conservative perceptions about the film's content involved several themes. The most prominent issue in the material was a concern over perceived defamation of Christ (seen being portrayed in the film as a liar, hypocrite, rationalizing wimp). One protest placard read, "Temptation's Jesus is a moral degenerate who fantasizes sex, a sinner who violates his own principles (Harmetz, "Temptation Sets" C14). Chuck Colson, commentator on *Focus on the Family* radio, said of the symbolic use of Jesus, "The film depicts Christ as a wacked out, lustful and confused wimp who says such things as 'Lucifer is inside me'" (*Oprah* 11/12/88). Jerry Falwell said of *Temptation*'s depiction of Jesus, "Hollywood has never stooped so low, it slanders, libels and ridicules the most central figure in Western history" (*Lutheran*). James Wall, editor for the *Christian Century*, a progressive Christian publication, was one of the few conservatives who saw the film and said, "Jesus is presented as driven by a God who makes strange demands of his followers" (8).

Such statements are demonstrative of an insecurity generated by the film within the religious conservative community. This insecurity is symbolized in the loss of power, illustrated in the image of Jesus as a "confused wimp." The disruption and inversion of traditional characteristics of Christ generated a wide range of reactionary language that, at some point, was turned on Scorsese and Universal.

Many points of contention developed over deeply buried issues about Jesus Christ. The film destabilized their well-established and unchallenged views by reopening a serious discussion about his humanity, his personality, his tendencies, and his role as savior. One of the most prominent areas of discussion was his sexuality. The film openly questions Jesus' sexual drives and introduces sexual desire into his thought processes and motivation. Religious conservatives railed against the idea that Jesus experienced sexual desires, overlooking perhaps the most original part of the film's message; that Jesus may have wanted to live like an ordinary man, get married, and have children.

The *Last Temptation*'s treatment of Jesus' sexuality called into question commonly accepted meanings and exposed oppositions and tensions present in society (Turner, *Ritual* 41). Father Vincent Miceli's editorial statement reflects the significance of violations and carnality elicited by the film: "This obsession with immoral sexual activity indicates that the makers of this abominable film are incapable of raising their mental fixations to any reality higher than the biological cravings for carnal pleasure to be obtained in any manner whatsoever" (qtd. in Congressional Record E 3433). Underlying this anxiety over Jesus' sexuality rests a theological subtext that the *Last Temptation* encourages a permissive lifestyle that threatens the survival of the nuclear family (Forshey 180).

Conservative anxiety was heightened by rumors about the film and Jesus' sexual lusting. This anxiety mixed with outrage when a copy of Paul Schrader's early script was circulated and read. This most prominently referred-to section was of great offense to religious conservatives. Jesus is in bed with Mary Magdalene:

JESUS: The road on which the mortal becomes immortal, God becomes human. I was so stupid. I tried to find a way outside my own flesh. I wanted crowds, great ideas, death. But now I know: a woman is God's greatest work. God sleeps between your legs. (81–82)

In the final line of this dialogue there is a direct reference to God dwelling in the female genitalia, a radical inversion of common associations of sacred and profane. It is highly unlikely that religious conservatives would accept this line as a legitimate reference to the physical proximity of God's act of procreation through woman, or that the sexual union could be interpreted as a divine activity.

For conservatives its meaning refers more directly to the confusion produced by antithetical language. God, from this view, does not have sex, nor is the domain of purity in any way connected to sexual functions of the body. Sexuality is a human impulse that occurs in the domain of the unclean that, in turn, produces guilt. Guilt is thus associated with human sexuality. This admission creates a separation between clean and unclean which must be reconciled through forms of blame. Thus religious conservatives launched formative attempts to discredit such ideas about Jesus' sexuality and render them harmless. The studio, by financing the film, had violated the moral boundary separating the religious and secular realms by its linguistic linkage of the holy Christ with profane ideas. For the religious conservative this commingling of sacred and profane could not be tolerated and increased efforts were launched to combat such associations. But when, as in this case, an offense has been taken, there is little or no hope for reconciliation. The victim is forced into a reactionary mode whereby the source of the threat is attacked without reservation and discredited by any means necessary.

Written during and shortly after the film's release, Rev. Larry Poland's book, *The Last Temptation of Hollywood,* demonstrates how the polluted object, Universal Studios, is ritually imitated through religious language and moral terms and then objectified in a language of alienation.

> For decades TV and movies producers have been progressively se-duced by the forbidden fruit. They were teased by its attractive-ness—and yielded by featuring the short skirts and tight sweaters of the fifties. They held back the leaves to see the apple more clearly—and yielded to the nudity of the Playboy generation, the sixties . . . They touched and fondled the fruit—and yielded to the porno film flood of the eighties. Hollywood's Eve, with some re-sidual naivete, bit into the fruit—and having yielded, turned mor-ally condemned practices into public spectacles, orgies, parades—even pride. (226)

Using biblical symbols and metaphor, Rev. Poland evokes strong images of transgression and sets out to explain how the contested moral ground of "God's unspoiled world" has been polluted by Hollywood. Erotic overtones betray a fixation with the profane qualities of the enemy dem-onstrating a dualistic interplay of religious taboos regarding sexuality and a fascination with them. The language associates Universal with low symbolic forms as an eroticized constituent of its own suppressed fantasy life (Stallybrass and White 5). That is to say, Rev. Poland's extreme negation of Universal's moral deviance produces moral cleansing. The verbal attack serves to reestablish boundaries between sacred and profane.

The religious conservative stylistic imitation of the opposition, Uni-versal, as an object of projected guilt, is a symbolic reworking of its own hierarchical instability in order to reestablish clear boundaries. In this way the source of societal uncertainty is no longer produced by the social segment itself, but, instead, by a foreign entity, Universal, which now bears little or no resemblance to an ethical organization. Rev. Poland is able to both express and redeem the civic motive—elevation of God—through the use of such scapegoating (223).

Rev. Poland mimics the thoughts and ideas of the blasphemer in highly stylized language. This strategy allows him to take on the persona of the evil other through distinctive application of profane language without himself becoming associated with them. His invective continues in his reworking of the contemporary adversary, and all those who live and work in the entertainment industry are turned into the biblical equivalent of Canaanites or other groups of ritually impure people. "Day after day, week after week, Hollywood plays with the temptation to profit from sleaze" (225). For religious conservatives like Poland, corruption and sin in the industry itself were easily developed as devices for the ritual alienation of the movie studio.

Other tactics were put into use in the verbal war against Universal. One of the more prominent devices was the claim that the studio was using unethical economic practices and was exploiting Christians to sell the film.[3] The Rev. Donald Wildmon claimed that the market, or the theater, was a breeding ground for evil and immoral acts: "MCA is controlled by non-Christians. They see the film as a controversial one, which will make them millions of dollars. Universal officials are willing to desecrate the life of Christ in order to make money" (Editorial). For the Rev. Wildmon, the market represents the intersection of corrupting incentives that exploit and degrade the Christian religion.

These themes are familiar and predictable; they echo the traditional moral arguments of the Christian tradition. They are plain to our understanding, in part, because they are part of a uniform and coherent moral code. Its argument against Universal and the film relies on the specific and concrete relationships between this code, behavior, and media content. Religious conservatives enter the discourse of popular film through this moral framework, claiming that film influences attitudes, values, and beliefs in ways that can be harmful.

RITUAL SCAPEGOATING AND ANTI-SEMITISM

The religious conservative language of scapegoating produces demonized and stylized images and impressions of Hollywood, Universal, Martin Scorsese, and Lew Wasserman. Even though each of these is demonized in its own way, Lew Wasserman is treated differently because of his Jewish heritage. Wasserman, the head of MCA, became a focus of anti-Semitic stereotypes.[4]

Jewish scapegoating is deeply entrenched in the language of Christianity and this study adds little to the expansive body of material dedicated to the subject. It is, however, worthwhile to provide a perspective on the relationship between religious conservative rhetoric of alienation and the Jewish involvement. The majority of attention was focused on other matters. For the most part, religious conservatives did not actively distinguish Wasserman as a specific target of blame because of his Jewishness. His involvement is viewed as part of a larger exploitation of Christian beliefs by non-Christians.

The most pronounced demonstration of anti-Semitic activity took place under the leadership of the Rev. R. L. Hymers, who burned Wasserman in effigy in front of his Beverly Hills home. Hymers reasoned that underneath the *Last Temptation*'s blasphemous portrayal was a Jewish hatred of Christians: "Wasserman fans Jewish hatred with Temptation, through his role. In releasing the film Wasserman puts himself in the position of ridiculing a religion in which he did not grow up. . . . We think Lew Wasserman should go back to being the nice old man who introduced the Pope last September" (L34).

For the Rev. Hymers, the judgment concerning Wasserman's role is established in his Jewishness and all of the stereotypical assumptions surrounding the term's use. The Rev. Hymers plays on these assumptions when he judges Wasserman for not knowing anything about Christianity, yet he himself claims to know everything of importance about Wasserman. His symbolic destruction of the studio head represents the ritualized public shaming of the studio head. Unfortunately for the Rev. Hymers, the burning of Wasserman in effigy failed to produce the desired effect. Instead, it brought criticism and disdain from his brethren who were unable to justify such a concrete linkage between the Jewish people and the film's content.

The logic of the Rev. Hymers' argument, although faulty, retained some degree of cogency within some conservative circles, in which Pat Robertson was included. Robertson reasoned that because Jewish organizations did not come out against the film, they were, indirectly, promoting it. In a series of written exchanges with Abraham H. Foxman, the national director of the Anti-Defamation League of B'nai B'rith, Robertson argued that Jewish forces had come down on the side of Universal: "In my estimation, The Last Temptation of Christ will be a great detriment to the framework of brotherhood that you and I and others have worked so very hard to bring about between Jews and Christians in America. I urge you to do everything you can to exercise your influence with Lew Wasserman and others at MCA to eliminate this affront to Christianity before the trouble begins" (qtd. in *Harper's Magazine* 22).

Even though the statement maintains a posture of courtesy and presents options, it is also evident that the object of blame is predetermined by an assumption Robertson shares with the Rev. Hymers about Jews. Robertson's letter makes no attempt to satisfy Foxman's request. Instead, he turns the argument back onto the Jewish leader, claiming it is Foxman who must make the recompense. Thus Robertson holds the Jewish leader responsible, indirectly, for the controversy. This demonstrates how the process of scapegoating finds its most notable and memorable object of blame through a language of retaliation.

CONCLUDING REMARKS

This chapter began by identifying scapegoating as a process whereby the two social segments studied applied a particular type of religious language to support their positions. Initially, each rhetorical position demonstrates a somewhat balanced relationship, a state of civil equilibrium in which issues are negotiated according to boundaries of a common discourse (Burke *Grammar* 407). The initial boundaries separating and defining the two became problematic when the language itself moved toward a ritualistic alienation of the opposing view. Universal and Valenti demonstrate this by implementation of exclusionary language and authoritarian appeals to a kind of "absolute freedom." Such language conveys an element of linguistic unification of progressive liberals against religious conservatives. As a result, a new principle of merger was produced from the reformulation of secular domains of social influence.

Correspondingly, religious conservative rhetoric moved from a defensive posture toward Universal, to one of highly stylized emotional language that concentrated on forms of objectification and labeling. Religious conservative scapegoating ended up relying heavily on the use of ritual profaning of the liberal progressive view. This achieved a kind of stylized transfer of the profane to the ritualized position of evil other that was suitable for destruction.

By shifting the focus to the perpetrators of the film they could remove from the debate unsavory or complicating elements of Christianity. By making a clear distinction between the world of true Christian doctrine and that of the offensive Scorsese film, religious conservatives were able to ignore any legitimate claims the film made about the Christ figure. Indeed, the film, as a religious document, could be identified simply as a heretical and marginalized movie that had little or no relevance to Christians of our time.

It is argued here that, over a period of 16 months, the writings of Bright, Wildmon, Mother Angelica, Universal Studios, and Jack Valenti, among others, demonstrated how boundaries between religious cultural orientations and their secular counterpart became more ritually alien to one another. The *Last Temptation* brought religious issues to the forefront of popular culture for meaningful debate that, in turn, engendered a breakdown between secular and religious structures at one point. At another point, it brought the reestablishment and refinement of the two moral languages. New principles arose out of these processes whereby the two segments purified their identities through the dialectic of scapegoating (Burke, *Grammar* 4).

NOTES

1. Hierarchy is a value-charged structure that, as William Rueckert points out, is simultaneously unifying and divisive (131).

2. Babbington and Evans note that the Christ film is a rare phenomenon "because of its severity and because it has obvious sub-generic limitations, incapable of variations like other genres. Thus, its limited output—four major films in over fifty years" (149).

3. The market is treated by Universal as a democratizing force—a place in which ideas are tested for their value to society. The market is commonly viewed as a neutral element because it is not considered to have a moral component. The locus of moral authority resides in a given transaction. The market is an invisible force that sanctions success. For this reason, Universal and Valenti never refer to the market as a moral arbiter.

4. There is a fourth area, one that is much less prominent and is raised primarily by the Jewish contingency of the protest. These leaders, Rabbi Haim Asa, Dennis Prager, and Michael Medved, make the claim that Hollywood nihilism is the source of the problem.

Chapter 5

PROTECTING FREEDOM OF SPEECH: SCAPEGOATING RELIGIOUS CONSERVATIVES

The resistance by religious conservatives to the secular use of the symbol Jesus, led to their adoption of a scapegoating strategy. The implementation of this ritual of blame provided a way to alleviate their anxieties and reestablish clear boundaries between themselves and a secular culture outside. In a similar way, Universal Studios, Scorsese, and their allies, merged in a common voice against religious conservatives. Universal and its supporters saw the religious conservative attack as a challenge to the sacred mandates of a free society. These voices adopted a language of scapegoating to alleviate their fears and reestablish the balance between religious and secular domains. Biographers, film reviewers, critics, and commentators used their mass-mediated venues to rebut religious conservatives and put forward a moral agenda of their own.

There are several components to this analysis. The first involves an examination of the director as an artistic type who carries the banner of artistic freedom. Biographers and critics, as well as reviewers, embrace Scorsese as a hero for their cause. The second involves an examination of the highly emotional language of the reviews of the film and the resemblance it bears to religious discourse. A third area examines ambiguities in the liberal progressive argument. The ideas consistent with rational dialogue seem to be important to proponents of free speech, yet such ideas are, at times, not put into practice in their arguments. Contradictions present in these texts point to failed logic, which, in turn, points toward underlying strategies of scapegoating.

Exaggeration is another common quality of the language of ritual alienation and several examples are studied here. Labels, stereotypes, and ridicule all provide verbal clues to the ways liberal progressives distinguish themselves from their opponents in ritualized blame. These forms produce a distinctive concentration of power that occurs when the liberal progressive language shifts from an essentially aesthetic, or therapeutic discourse of film criticism and commentary, to one that is charged with religious symbols and imagery (Carter 122).

Finally, beneath all these rhetorical strategies is the social hierarchy itself that is examined directly, through the dialectic of free speech and censorship. For liberal progressives the threat of censorship is a serious one met with firm resistance, at times adopting a language that is antithetical to the principles of their position concerning free speech. These inconsistencies are insightful evidence for examining how scapegoating functions as a critique of free speech arguments.

The textual material discussed here represents a cross-section of 60 nonreligious sources that include biographical material, film reviews, and commentaries that are examined for similarities and differences. Most of this material was published around the time of the film's release, although the biographical sources come from a later period. Generally, these voices point out how the controversy masks, distracts, or draws attention from the film's aesthetic value and purpose. Their treatment of the film's religious content focuses on a number of areas: the acknowledgement of the director's sincerity and dedication as well as his artistic genius, an account of the strengths and weaknesses of the film, the comparison of *Temptation* to Scorsese's other films, the comparison with other films of the genre, the examination of incidental information about the project, anecdotal information about the film and its director.

MARTIN SCORSESE—THE ARTISTIC GENIUS

Biographers and critics commonly characterize Scorsese as an original artist driven to create original film art that reaches audiences on a deeper level than most Hollywood films (Kelly, Keyser, Thompson, Ehrenstein and others). These authors give serious attention to his religious and artistic motivation, and consider his vision as one of a marginalized person—the position of the true artist. As a misunderstood visionary these writers orient Scorsese as outside the cultural institutions of the time.

For the most part, biographers reconstruct the film's director as a particular kind of marginal figure who is fighting for recognition and acceptance in a world that misunderstands his work. His soul-searching, unorthodox study of the Christ figure was evidence that he was following in the footsteps of other great artists who used their craft to break through the false consciousness of bad art (Jensen 366). His marginal status in the Church, his challenge to the status quo, and his artistic vision, were key ingredients in their characterizations of Scorsese as an artistic genius.

Because he was viewed as a rebel and religious outsider, Scorsese gained a great deal of appeal and currency in the community of biographers, film critics, reviewers, peers, and writers, who lauded him for his courage in challenging traditional religious views. This elevation of Scorsese's status is made evident by analyzing a variety of biographical materials and reviews, and their meritorious discussion of Scorsese and his work. In line with the historic view of the role of the artist in visionary transformer of society, these writers are compelled to defend and valorize the director.

To these defenders, Scorsese's blasphemous film is rendered unique and innovative because it challenges the mainstream view and pushes the limits of film art. Almost uniformly, biographers and critics speak positively about Scorsese because his films challenge the status quo of mindless Hollywood entertainment. To them, the fact that the *Last Temptation* was met by religious conservatives with great anger and retribution was evidence of his currency as a great filmmaker. These supporters identified with Scorsese's marginality and noncompliance. For them, Scorsese and his film served as vehicles by which they, as marginal figures, could ignite their creative impulse and ingenuity, and somehow, in the mundane moments of the weekly film review, become mythic figures, themselves loved or hated for their symbolic features and loyalties.

In the face of great pressure over *Temptation,* film critics and reviewers defended Scorsese and his original Christ film. For example, critic and reviewer Christopher Sharrett asserts that conservatives fail to appreciate the depth of the film and its director. "The vicious attacks on the filmmaker have served to obscure and deflect the reasoned investigation LTOC tries, falteringly but with considerable integrity, to undertake" (28). Hal Hinson of the *Washington Post* took the work as a profound statement of the director's religious sincerity. "It is a work of great seriousness by one of this country's most gifted filmmakers" (B1). Mike McGrady of *Newsday* applauded Scorsese for having the "courage" to challenge the prevailing filmic representations of Jesus. "It may be Scorsese's most courageous film and it is technically superb" (3). Sheila Bensen of the *Los Angeles Times* treats Scorsese as a hero for his valiant attempt to bring the biblical story into the context of the contemporary culture and make it fresh, new, and relevant for audiences. "At the bottom of the controversy is an intense, utterly sincere, frequently fascinating piece of art by a director for whom, clearly, the message of Jesus' life has immediacy and meaning" (3.5). Yes, the film was blasphemous and offensive, but, as Michael Medved pointed out after his advanced viewing of the film, most reviewers were intent on supporting Scorsese.

> I told them [the press] it is the height of irony that all this controversy should be generated by a film that turns out to be so breathtakingly bad, so unbearably boring. . . . I was therefore amazed and appalled in the days that followed at the generally respectful—even reverential—tone that so many of my colleagues adopted in their reviews. In particular, I found it impossible to understand the one critic who had snorted the loudest and clucked the most derisively at the afternoon screening we both attended, but whose ultimate report to the public featured glowing praise and only the most minor reservations. . . . When I called him to ask about the contrast between his privately expressed contempt and his on-the-record admiration, he proved surprisingly candid in explaining his inconsistency. "Look, I know the picture's a dog. We both know that, and probably Scorsese knows it too. But with all Christian crazies shooting at him from every direction, I'm not going to knock him in public" (49).

The language of film critics, as well as biographers, operates within the parameters of scapegoating defined by rituals of inclusion and exclusion—linguistic patterns of maintaining community. It makes little difference whether or not the religious conservative arguments are valid, because these writers saw in them a threat and thus mounted a defense of Scorsese—the type for their own rite of passage to the sublime. To this end, and ironically so, Scorsese became a religious voice for film critics who viewed Jesus as much more of a Nietzchean superman than a resurrected God of the Christian religion (Babbington 151). Likewise, film critics saw Scorsese's *Last Temptation* as important to the 1980s, largely because his message was not that of mainstream Hollywood and provided a desired correction to previous movies of the genre. Scorsese serves, for these voices, as a kind of messiah who proved once again that film could serve a grander purpose than raw entertainment—it could ignite and restore their utopian ideals.

The same writers tend to ignore the relationship between Scorsese's various religious impressions and normative Christian paradigms concerning the theological issues swirling around the *Last Temptation*. The elision is significant because Scorsese's religious consciousness, which biographers and critics refer to as important to the positive impulse of his film, involves contradictory statements by him that remain largely unexamined. This is to say that these voices tend to accept Scorsese's religious convictions at face value. They also generally assume that common elements in the *Last Temptation* narrative, and the underlying religious purposes, are a matter of "personal" expression and serve simply to validate the artist's right to creative freedom and have no implicit role in shaping the Church's identity. It is highly likely that their identification with Scorsese as an artist supports their underlying skepticism toward institutionalized power of all forms, particularly those of the Christian persuasion.

The reasoning behind their arguments in support of the film are often faulty, because Scorsese's defenders' work is not about providing valid explanations for the film's controversial reception; it is rather, about art and crafting images and ideas that embellish, exaggerate, and entice an audience in a therapeutic tangle. Their work is drama, a play on meaning whose significance, as forms of rhetorical scapegoating, rests in the inversions created. Nowhere is this therapeutic tangle more recognizable than in the various assessments of the film itself.

DEMONIZING RELIGIOUS CONSERVATIVES

Reviewers, film critics and editorial writers around the country took up Scorsese's cause and talked about the film in religious terms—as a testimony of personal faith. To some extent, liberal progressives adopted the language of the Christian religion and applied what appears to be a religious rhetoric of scapegoating. The more dispassionate discourse of film aesthetics was abandoned for a highly charged language of blame. Countless reviews and commentaries adopted this strategy to rebut and discount all conservative claims about the film in a battle against what appeared to be rigid intolerance. In the context of these diatribes the film became at once a correct religious interpretation of the Bible and an irrefutable representation of free expression.

It is unlikely that reviewers and commentators had any idea that they had, in these diatribes, linked two seemingly incompatible worlds, the world of Christian fundamentalism and the rational world of free speech. Nevertheless, as this chapter points out, the liberal progressive arguments took on the tone and language of religion and used religious claims to rebut and invalidate the opposing view in a what could be considered a form of secular fundamentalism. It may seem quite a stretch to argue that film critics were intolerant "fundamentalists" but when one studies the rhetoric and the logic and the ambiguity present in their statements it becomes more and more clear that the film's vocal defenders used the rhetoric of blame to neutralize the religious conservative threat and strengthen their own cultural status. This study now examines notable linguistic patterns and characteristics present in reviews and commentaries as they contribute to the scapegoating of the religious conservative position. It is asserted here that the arguments that support Scorsese's film and the free speech position rely on a rhetoric of scapegoating to cope with threats of censorship and unify their own view (Burke, *Grammar* 409).[1]

Scapegoating as a form of argument draws on familiar modes of communication; it is characterized by highly emotional language and exaggeration (Girard 19). It relies on all types of logical fallacy, stereotyping being the most obvious. Beyond this, we find in these statements reactionary terms and a zeal that mirrors the polemical material produced by religious conservatives. Textual examples provide verbal clues to the ways in which liberal progressives distinguish themselves from their opponents in a process of ritualized blame. The combined result is a distinctive concentration of power that occurs when the liberal progressive language shifts from an essentially aesthetic, or therapeutic discourse of film criticism and commentary, to one that is charged with name-calling and blame (Carter 122).[2]

The reviews discussed here represent a cross-section of 50 nonreligious sources that are examined for similarities and differences. These reviews of *Last Temptation* were printed at around the time of the film's release on August 12, 1988. Generally they point out how the controversy masks, distracts, or draws attention from the film's aesthetic value and purpose. Their treatment of the film's religious content focuses on a number of areas: the acknowledgment of the director's sincerity and dedication, an account of the strengths and weaknesses of the film, the comparison of *Temptation* to Scorsese's other films, the comparison with other films of the genre, the examination of incidental information about the project, anecdotal information about the film and its director, as well as aesthetic elements.

Richard Corliss's review in *Film Comment* demonstrates the prevalent attitude among film reviewers who countered the religious conservative opposition. The review mixes the language of the sacred with that of the profane in an assertion that the problem stems not from the film's content but from the profane imaginings of religious conservatives. "Some fundamentalists think the film is about the messiah having sex with all those fabulous Biblical babes. Perhaps they would call it *Jesus Fucking Christ. None of the above*" ("Body and Blood" 34). Corliss's use of profanity has a certain shock value and it creates an image that scandalizes the traditional view of Jesus. This scandalous element is produced in both literal and figurative ways. In the literal sense the reference to "fucking" is directly linked to images of the film and Jesus' sexual activity. In the figurative sense, the word refers to the common vernacular curse, the base and vulgar language that negates the conservative interpretation of Jesus' identity.

This highly charged language also provides a mechanism for the linguistic destabilization of traditional relations between the church and a secular culture. Corliss's suggested hypothetical title achieves this through parody of the traditional image associations and by contradicting the formal relations between profane and sacred. The basic function of the title is to invert language structures, creating ambiguity in order to reconstruct the historic figure, Jesus Christ, as a nonreligious icon. The figure's traditional meaning is scandalized through figurative language and an allusion to his imagined sexual activity.

In another section of his review Corliss levels an attack on conservative reasoning, asserting that attempts of conservatives to demonize the source of evil are foolish. In it Corliss adopts the religious language of Christian faith in order to discredit traditional Christian views. He distinguishes a correct religious view from the more base views of religious conservatives by using stereotypes:

> Only a born-again paranoid could see a conspiracy of Jewish Christ-killers from a movie directed and produced by Italian Catholics and written by a Dutch Calvinist and a Presbyterian. And only a theological despot would demand that a movie be compatible with his or anyone else's religion. (34)

The phrases "born-again paranoid" and "theological despot" produce an extreme alienation of the conservative religious view, which becomes charged with negative meaning. The language separates the high moral position of Corliss from the illegitimate claims of religious conservatives. After his debunking of religious conservatives for incorrectly interpreting events, Corliss makes a rather bold claim that Scorsese's Jesus is *the* Jesus of the New Testament. He supports this assertion by relating several aspects of Christian religion in its true state to the film's content.[3] For example, Corliss asserts that it is because Scorsese's Jesus is a human being who struggles that the religious dimensions in the film come to life and produce a legitimate redemptive message needed for a secular culture:

> This is a Jesus who spans the millennia. And the final proof of *The Last Temptation*'s message is that it has greater numbers of the non-religious thinking and arguing seriously about Jesus than a snake-shaking fundamentalist could dream of. It's a Billy Graham Crusade for the lapsed Christian. (42)

Corliss reworks religious language and thought to fit a new religious premise, one that has a particular emphasis on the autonomy of the individual and one that negates traditional, or religious conservative, views of community. This is achieved by an odd combining of secular with religious language in Corliss's personal testimony, which draws two discourses into a unified polemic in which a new secularized Christianity can emerge. Corliss creates this new Christianity by sacrificing the old "snake-shaking fundamentalist"—the polluted agent of distorted ideas about Jesus—to the ethical machinery of his free society of ideas.

Scorsese's portrayal of Jesus appeals to Corliss because it presents religious ideas without religiosity. He liked the film because it has no self-evident structural arrangements of religion associated with traditional institutions. It allows the individual viewer freedom to discern without the pressures of an organized doctrine. There are no religious requirements of ritual inclusion to which he need adhere, only his personal beliefs. In this way, the *Last Temptation* eliminates problems associated with what Corliss calls "theological despotism" of conservative Christianity by stripping away the symbols of a church hierarchy so that religion may exist as a personal entertainment experience. This view is echoed in other reviews, which celebrate the autonomy of Jesus' individual conscience to discern right from wrong outside the context of organized religious doctrine.

Corliss's argument gains its strength, in part, from its contradictory quality—the inherent incongruities that occur when religious claims co-exist with the appeals of free speech. For example, Corliss readily, and vehemently, defends a particular religious view while at the same time he attacks formal Christian religion for being against free expression. This contradiction can be partially explained by recognizing that Corliss's application of religious language operates to achieve dominance over the opposing view. He endorses religious ideas in order to discount, burlesque, and mock formal religion itself and to separate from, and elevate, his form of religion. Corliss and others, then, apply religious language, as the charged emotional material that reinforces the ethical negative of the secular order—it functions primarily to exclude religion from the sacred mandates of a free society.

In many cases reviewers make inaccurate claims about the film's religious content in order to counter religious conservative concerns. For example, Christopher Sharrett's review in *Cineaste* asserts that there is a natural connection between the *Last Temptation* and the Gospels of the Bible. "It is the only English-language film to challenge the premises of the institutional church while still working within the framework of the Gospels (the real source for Scorsese and Schrader rather than the god-awful Kazantzakis novel)" (3.3). Here Sharrett claims to have authoritative knowledge concerning the content of the film as it reflects theological and biblical material. His language portrays a sense of sincerity and sobriety that is compelling and his parenthetical carefully clarifies the textual relations between the film and the Bible. Unfortunately, his statements are inaccurate. The film is much more faithful to Kazantzakis's novel than to the Bible. The *Last Temptation* narrative only loosely follows biblical accounts and, for the most part, departs radically from them. For example, the opening scene follows the book's opening with Jesus writhing on the ground in a nightmare/hallucination. Nowhere in the Gospels are there any such a portrayals of the Christ figure. Sharrett's assertion betrays a rhetorical strategy aimed at invalidating existing assumptions concerning the Christ figure in an attempt to make the religious conservative sound heretical and extreme. In quite unusual posturing Sharrett sounds like a biblical authority. In terms of scapegoating, the underlying rhetorical purpose is not to correct the reader's understanding of the film but to refute an opposing force by using the tools of religious discourse. His rebuttal has at its core the assumption that the film itself is a sacred text of protected speech. The *Last Temptation* is taken as a pure act of free speech, an irrefutable form of religious truth.

Stanley Kauffman adopts a similar strategy in the *New Republic*. He writes, "The protesters against worldliness of this film ignore the fact that its conclusion emphasizes the transcendence of the spirit over the flesh" (28). Kauffman's claim is incorrect. Scorsese leaves this issue up to viewer speculation as the film ends with Jesus' death on the cross, not with his resurrection. One is prompted to ask on what grounds does Kauffman enter a purely religious debate if not to invoke some adherence to a view of the film as a pure act of free speech? By acknowledging this possibility one also can reconcile the contradictions. There is no intended religious conviction here, or desire to forward a religious argument. The language is used to solidify the film's legitimacy as free speech—the sacred doctrine of liberalism.

The language in such statements also helps position these reviewers squarely against religious conservatives in an "us versus them" posturing that solidifies the reviewer's sense of identify and belonging. It makes little difference to Kauffman, Sharrett, and Corliss whether their theology is valid because the use of religious language, and its primary symbol, "Jesus," are part of a rhetorical strategy whereby a set of religious ideas themselves may be marginalized in order to elevate the social grouping to which the reviewers belong.

David Denby adopts this position of moral superiority in a *New York* magazine article. In his full-force invective against conservatives Denby protests, "I don't think the film is blasphemous but I'm not surprised that some people are enraged. Certainly anyone devoted to maintaining Christ as a lacquered benevolent spirit in a Disneyland of happiness is not going to like this movie . . . " (50).[4] A tone of sarcasm and skepticism permeates Denby's review as he depicts religious conservatives as demented, otherworldly people uncomfortable with the realities of contemporary American society. The review, in this sense, holds up the film as a realistic presentation of Jesus and his moral universe—one that despises formal Christian religion. Talking down to religious conservatives, Denby reduces their issues of concern to their simplest or most harmless forms, thus making the claims appear to be absurd and unfounded. "That most of the protesters seem almost wholly concerned with the sex scene only goes to show the infantile level of most modern-day Christian activism" (7). Like Corliss and Sharrett, Denby diverts the debate away from the film itself to focus on the religious conservatives themselves emphasizing their marginalized status in the broader culture.

SCAPEGOATING AS FREE SPEECH

Reviewers used their columns to set out new moral terms for the argument by which they could vindicate Scorsese and Universal as well as promote the film as an idealized representation of free speech. As these textual examples demonstrate, in most cases reviewer arguments are shaped by the adoption of religious language. Religious rhetoric is called on not as a means to examine the film's content but primarily to discredit an opposing view and set that view up as antithetical to free speech.

Rebuttals of religious conservative protests are combined with a language of condescension in John Hopkins's review found in the *New Statesman and Society*. In this essay Hopkins discounts the religious conservative protest by trivializing their concerns: "The Bible provides answers and order, and the demonstrators want it unchallenged and uncomplicated. . . . Did Scorsese push the film beyond the boundaries of good taste, thus provoking the uproar? The answer is 'no.' If only because the questions are irrelevant" (39). Hopkins's refutation of religious conservative concerns is tactical, part of a larger repudiation of the religious conservative claims in order to place a secular order above the religious social hierarchy (Lawton 32). It is true that the issue of good taste Hopkins refers to is a matter of personal interpretation. One cannot, however, simply say that Hopkins and the others are merely voicing personal opinions. They operate within a larger system that sanctions their values and ideas. Combined, the media voice of these reviewers comprises a substantial force and influence on the public.

Another of these influential voices, Pam Cook of the *Monthly Film Bulletin,* launches an impersonal yet potent refutation of religious conservatives in her review of the film. "The objections on the grounds of sex are clearly a red herring: of the two sex scenes, one shows Jesus as a non-participant observer in Mary Magdalene's brothel, followed by his refusal of her invitation to stay . . . " (287). Cook, like Sharrett and Kauffman, adopts a biblical argument that affirms the film's religious statement. She presses her polemic home by turning the argument back onto religious conservatives, charging that the Christian Church is itself the source of "perverse and contradictory impulses":

> Those who, sight unseen, cry blasphemy have nevertheless got it right. Scorsese and Schrader have produced a deeply transgressive view of religion which at the very least opens it up for general discussion beyond the protective confines of the church, and at the most unmasks the perverse and contradictory impulses at the heart of Christian faith. (287)

The language in this statement inverts the religious moral order and the rules and mandates commonly associated with it seeking to make a marginalized view of Christ the dominant view. By arguing for a new moral order Cook takes up the role of revolutionary religious reformer. The rhetoric inverts the assumed relationship between religion and secular language producing a kind of moral absolute of a secular nature. At its core is a claim to ultimate authority—religious moral truths are synonymous with free speech acts. Like Corliss, Hopkins, Denby, Sharrett, and

Kauffman, Cook redefines Christ according to the philosophical mandates of a worldview that defends Scorsese's free-speech rights. These rights are seen as inseparable from the artistic creation that itself takes on the status of an absolute truth (as in the Bible).

Correspondingly, the reason one finds such reviews simultaneously endorsing the film's religious message at the same time they deny traditional religious values is because these reviews in no way associate the use of religious discourse with the practice of religion. The function, or practical outcome, of the argument is simply to displace the religious view by challenging its correctness while correspondingly denying any religious intent. The scapegoat exists within this skewed logic and in the ultimate aim—the ritual purgation of a particular religious form of free speech.

As I have demonstrated here, Denby, Sharrett, Cook, Kauffman, Hopkins, and Corliss discuss religious ideas as authorities of religion, not because they are religious but because their right of free expression demands they take the high moral ground in defense of Universal Studios, Martin Scorsese, and the sacred mandates of free speech. Their position is derived through the demonstrated weakness of the opposition's view concerning the film's content. Through these weaknesses reviewers are able to ritualistically alienate religious conservative ideas and concerns from the dialogue, setting them up as sacrificial scapegoats—banished from the realm of free speech.

As film critics compare and contrast themselves with religious conservatives, they seize on the outward differences, such as the spiritual, the religious and the moral, as rhetorical tools for self-definition. Their relationship to this agenda develops through terms and phrases, which define them according to what they oppose. Reviewers exonerate the *Last Temptation* not because it is a good film but because they find good reasons to identify and ally themselves with Scorsese and Universal. They gather in a common social allegiance around the social hierarchy of free speech which, we could say, calls for enlistment to Universal's cause. Its adherents are bound to support the ideal not as an inclusive domain of pluralism but as the supreme structure—as an absolute claim to a moral good. Their friendly treatment of Scorsese and his film operates primarily as a defense of a liberal progressive hierarchy premised on absolute claims of freedom of speech.

CENSORSHIP AND SCAPEGOATING

Fear of censorship provides the linguistic engine, which drives the process of ritual scapegoating in its various forms. The threat of censorship produces the language that pulls the various disparate views together to fight a common enemy of free speech. Issues of censorship represent the unspoken force in all of the reviews studied here. Corliss, for example, does not explain his basis for attacking and discrediting the religious conservative protest. He assumes the right to do so because conservatives represent the powers of censorship.

The term "censorship" clusters around the language of moral imperatives such as Valenti's use of "absolute right."[5] It is always used, in the cases studied here, as a tool for separating good and evil, right and wrong, high and low, and so forth (Burke, *Religion* 201). Censorship implies a subset of opposites that mutually balance one another in a process of scapegoating—referring to the ordered relations where insiders and outsiders are located and defined. Beyond this, censorship has historical qualities revealed in the ongoing struggle on the part of filmmakers who seek to innovate and break new ground. In the cases cited here reviewers and commentators call on familiar anxieties and fears associated with previous encounters to support their arguments. For this reason there is no need for reviewers to discuss the nature and meaning of censorship or whether or not fundamentalists pose an actual threat. It is enough to simply invoke the idea and out come all of the associated fears and anxieties.

The popular film critic Roger Ebert develops his comments about the film around the issue of censorship. He asks, "Why is it that censors always seem to attack the serious works of art and ignore the trivial ones? . . . I believe it is because self-appointed censors fear only those films that make people think" (26). Ebert continues, "If I were a theologian I might be tempted myself—tempted to suggest that these censors are themselves committing heresy by attempting to fashion an image of Christ that denies his manhood" (26). For Ebert, it is a foregone conclusion that religious conservatives have no sense of the artistic value of the *Last Temptation*. Their action is, to Ebert, simply another example of the backward thinking of religious conservatives who seek to snuff out differences of opinion. The central kernel of Ebert's rebuttal resides in the reference to censorship; the term invokes numerous references to anti-free speech activity in its most important sense while invoking the characteristics of censorship in its language. Ebert's negation of the religious conservative view, in a strange way, also negates free speech.

Editorial writers and commentators add their perspectives to the furor; many are vociferous in their attacks on religious conservatives as censors. They defend Scorsese's artistic freedom and support the film's message as a symbol of free speech. Charles Champlin, arts editor for the

Los Angeles Times, asserts that free expression is the aspect of society, which defines a civilized people from undeveloped cultures. "In spite of all that history has taught us, we continue to use suppression and censorship to cleanse and protect" (6.1). Champlin reasons that there are important differences between "what is distasteful and what is dangerous" in free speech. "If Martin Scorsese's film had somehow infringed on anybody's right to believe in Christ, the protesters would have had a point, but it didn't" (6.1). Champlin chides religious conservatives for not having any awareness of what the film is about, and for infringing on others' rights to see the film. He denies the legitimacy of the religious conservative argument by asserting that movies are inherently amoral objects of study and therapy. Movies do not infringe on people's rights; they are simply escapist entertainment. Champlin makes it very clear that ideas themselves are not threatening, while at the same time, reacting to religious conservative statements as if they were dangerous.

The point is not to argue that the religious conservative threat was not real but to point out that the currency of the charge about censorship is based on perception rather than fact.[6] These writers were reacting emotionally. They were not making sound logical arguments but engaging in a process of scapegoating whereby the opposition was elevated to a status of an almost insurmountable foe that had to be faced, then defeated through the use of stereotyping, mockery, ritual inversion, and ambiguous language. Their arguments concerning the film are wrapped in the defense of the right of free expression that transforms the film into a symbol, an enactment of freedom that is inherently moral (the highest principle known to Americans). These voices are clear in their declarations about free speech—the polar opposite of censorship. But they go beyond this declaration to celebrate free expression as an absolute right of Scorsese and Universal regardless of the film's religious content.

In his *Orange County Register* editorial, Bob Emmers argues for free speech while speaking in terms of moral absolutes. For Emmers the main issue is not the offensive content of a film but a recurring problem in American society—religion seeking to suppress free expression. "Let's suppose for a minute that the movie is more or less blasphemous, whatever that means. . . . So what? I still ought to be able to go see it without a bunch of holier-than-thou twits telling me it's not good for me" (B1). Emmers proclaims his independence of thought and action in defiance of protesting religious conservatives. He exercises this freedom by going to a movie theater, the location where free speech abounds. Indeed, the theater is viewed by Emmers and the others mentioned here as the protective domain of democracy.

Mike Duffy of the *Detroit Free Press* tackles the subject with similar name-calling. "They're back. The know-nothings have found a new cause. They always do" (12). Duffy's highly emotional language is exemplified in a string of labels describing the protesting Christians: "know-nothings, ignoramus faction, fun-loathing people, wacky pack" (12). His piece is punctuated with sarcasm and ridicule as Duffy seeks to reinforce the perception that conservative Christians are intellectual primitives who rail against the civilizing forces of American culture. "Anti-intellectual, anti-freedom of speech, anti-Semitic, you name it and there are some know-nothings who practice it" (12). For Duffy it is the character and beliefs of religious conservatives that are on trial because they stand for all that is against freedom. Labels and stereotypes litter the emotionally charged rhetoric of Duffy's commentary. "This time they're raising a ruckus over the *Last Temptation of Christ.* The American ignoramus faction is perpetually geeked up on self-righteous bile. It always needs fresh meat. Fresh meat and fear. Fresh meat and intolerance." (12). The terms are quite vivid and plain in their meaning—conjuring images of carnivorous animals killing and feeding on innocent film directors.

This advocate of free speech achieves his goal by positioning religious conservatives in the role of alien other, who may be sacrificed as the scapegoat for the failures of a secular value system that claims openness and inclusion. Emmers and Duffy operate under the assumption that all people should share a common attitude of openness and tolerance toward differences of opinion, yet, ironically, they themselves employ a rhetoric of intolerance. The rationale of these arguments is conditioned through scapegoating a process whereby liberal progressives become impervious to the concerns of religious conservatives because of their own narrow perspective of those they oppose. Critics that argue for the unfettered rights of a film to blaspheme are in effect campaigning for the right to selectively offend the members of those they disagree with, namely religious conservatives, by abusing their religious beliefs (Webster 59).

Religious conservatives are "dangerous censors" who want to "dictate what we can watch" argues the *Playboy* commentator Michael McWilliams (46). McWilliams's review poses the same question as Emmers, Sharrett, and Ebert, "Why not wait until the finished pic is released? Why attempt to enforce pre-censorship, which is basically alien to the American way of life? Constitutionally, there is freedom of speech, no matter how unpalatable" (8). The final sentence in the quote clarifies that for McWilliams issues over the content of the film are less important than matters of power. What McWilliams is telling conservatives is, in essence, "Whether you like it or not, that's the law."

Duffy, Emmers, and McWilliams bring to the surface odd and often contradictory elements concerning ideas about openness and tolerance that are essential to the concept of free speech. For example, the arguments against censorship, one would assume, apply to society in general and all kinds of expression of views and so forth. In many cases, however, this open-ended and tolerant perspective is not produced or promoted in the liberal progressive claims. The texts studied here tend to invoke the language of censorship primarily as a strategy of ritual scapegoating—that is, to push certain forms of expression out of the arena of free speech. This is an interesting and important persuasive device that is embedded in liberal progressive rebuttals of religious conservative views.

These writers demonstrate in their reviews and commentaries that their arguments are not really about free speech. Instead, they are about the lawful endorsement of a particular kind of speech to the exclusion of the speech upheld by others. Reviewers, critics, and commentators mentioned here are actually transferring to the question of Scorsese's right to free expression the same kind of rigor and the same kind of blind zeal that the most militant kind of Christian fundamentalists bring to the exposition of their own holy scriptures (Webster 59). Liberal progressives have applied to the right of free speech the same fixed mentality as their fundamentalist neighbors apply to the Bible. They end up defending the *Last Temptation* with the same kind of fervor that religious conservatives bring to their defense of scriptures (59). It is natural, then, that progressives are enraged when conservatives find any part of Scorsese's film blasphemous, just as much as a proposal to delete certain portions of the Gospels would enrage Christian fundamentalists.

CONCLUDING REMARKS

The texts analyzed here invoke the discourse of scapegoating as a response to a felt threat of censorship. The coping mechanisms used by free speech advocates trigger a language of blame and retribution aimed at those who present the greatest degree of insecurity—conservative Christians. It is argued here that such positions, when viewed through the scapegoat motif, reveal structural relations between competing and exclusionary social hierarchies. Within these hierarchies reside the ethical sanctions, rules, and laws that maintain order. The breakdown of orderly social relations occurs when the process of scapegoating begins and proceeds, unabated, to a point of extreme negation of the opposing group in whom the scapegoat is fully manifest.

The movement through this process also causes uncertainty for both factions and results in the linguistic breakdown of a moral discourse to provide explanations and answers. The segments at risk attempt to re-establish their distinctive positions by dissociating themselves from the source of social wrongdoing. The end result is guilt reduction in the banished scapegoat who produces a refined, more thoroughly fixed structural relation between social groups in reified ethical mandates concerning inclusion and exclusion.

These texts demonstrate how scapegoating became a fundamental part of the rhetorical language of biographers, reviewers, film critics, and commentators around the time of the film's release. The language used by these participants is an indicator of a state or condition of affliction that is ascribed to all that cannot fulfill the expectations of the ethical mandates—free speech is an ethical ideal. The scapegoat is needed precisely because none can live up to the ideals of this mandate. But one can find a suitable object on which to place the blame for the collective failings to achieve this ideal and thus remove the guilt associated with such failure. The liberal progressive language examined here achieves a symbolic separation from the source of their collective guilt, identified as the various forms of the conservative branch of the Christian Church, Catholic and Protestant. Achieving this task allows for a renewal of the mandates of free speech and the social hierarchy for which it stands.

Perhaps the *Last Temptation* represents, for its supporters, a valorous attempt to stamp a redemptive signature on the culture of the 1980s, a time when grand ideals were fragmenting and the liberal agenda was losing its vigor and vision. Ironically, the film's redefinition of Christ was probably the single uniting theme among these voices. Even so, when taken as a counterreligious movement, the unified voice behind the *Last Temptation* fell to more earthly demands of movie moneymaking or to a vapid idealism. Such a movement could not be sustained in either the secular atmosphere of skepticism or the religious environment of retribution.

The *Last Temptation* conflict developed around moral sanctions about good versus evil, whereby one segment sought to maintain its identity by obscuring the other's view. This is the case with both positions discussed in this, and the previous chapter. In order for religious conservatives successfully to maintain their identity in a secular society, they felt a need to reduce the film and its supporters to powerless objects whereby their views and legitimate claims to free expression were reduced to their most vulgar characteristics—greed, lust, licentiousness, and so forth.

Correspondingly, Scorsese's defenders on the other side tended to obscure religious conservative concerns and generally failed to recognize or acknowledge that they had taken up a type of religious rhetoric to defend a free-speech premise (Turner, *From Ritual* 38). Legitimate claims about the content of the film and Universal's impropriety were trivialized by these voices, whereby religious conservatives were reduced to their most threatening and vulgar characteristics—religious fanatics, fundamentalists, draconian censors, and so forth.

This study suggests that the cultural contest over the *Last Temptation* and its meaning gave way, not to more open and enlightened dialogue but to hardened mechanisms of alienation, ritual scapegoat, and symbolic removal of the objectified other. It is not precisely clear to what degree these developments reflect a changed social landscape. What can be inferred, however, is that the principal relationships between religious organizations and liberal progressives changed (43). They have evolved into structures, which are increasingly exclusionary of the other.

NOTES

1. The term is used here primarily as a descriptive tool that refers to the collective voices that support the free speech position.

2. Free speech, as it is examined here, refers to the social hierarchy, which buttresses the liberal progressive position.

3. Corliss's statement at the end hints at a kind of personal conversion. If this is the case, then the rebuttal in the body of his argument is a confession of faith.

4. The terms "lacquered, benevolent, Disneyland" resemble terminology used by Scorsese himself, whose dominant image for the Catholic Church institution is "plastic dashboard Jesus" (Scorsese 3).

5. Jack Valenti is the primary industry spokesperson.

6. Economics, not censorship of the film, was the real issue concerning its availability. The film was released, initially in 12 cities, then to 36 more and later ran in selected theaters across the country. Universal's marketing strategy involved a short run, limited release of the film.

Chapter 6

APPEALS TO TOLERANCE: *OPRAH*'S PRESENTATION OF THE CONTROVERSY

By the time the *Last Temptation* reached theaters it was headline news. In the two weeks following the film's release a great deal of press attention was focused on the controversy. Newspapers covered events, and television picked up the subject and dedicated coverage to the issues on a wide range of news and entertainment programs.[1] This electronic coverage provided a dynamic setting in which ideas, issues, and concerns could be expressed and aired before millions of viewers. Among these programs were *Morton Downey, Jr., Sonya Live, Crossfire, Nightline, 20/20,* and the *MacNeil/Lehrer News Hour.* The popular daytime talk show, *Oprah,* also dedicated a program to the subject.

The *Oprah Winfrey* talk show provides an excellent showcase for presenting the opposing views as they played out in a public debate. The program delivers a kind of national electronic town square—a gathering place where ideas and issues about the film were debated in a face-to-face encounter. Scapegoating has been referred to in this study primarily as a linguistic phenomenon. Here the scapegoat motif is applied to the televisual language of the daytime talk show and examines Oprah Winfrey's August 14, 1988, program as it contributed to the film's defense. There are correlations between the processes of blame explored in the previous two chapters and the *Oprah* program examined here. There are similar concerns, similar arguments, and similar results.

Three methodological criteria will be emphasized. First, the talk show is premised on a problem/solution formula, which operates here as the context for ritual alienation of the guests. This formula provides the foundation from which other developments concerning scapegoating arise. The program content and set design, guest selection, and interaction contribute to this entertainment formula. Second, talk shows like *Oprah* require what Robin Anderson calls a "privatization" of social issues in order for personal concerns about religion to become a "voyeuristic" form of entertainment. Thus the form also tends to alienate, or disenfranchise, participants in order to satisfy viewers. Anderson observes: "Talk shows speak with a therapeutic language that examines only a privatized landscape of human experience, further rupturing individual needs from collective solutions. Instead of understanding and knowledge, television talk offers its viewers the voyeuristic pleasure of gazing into the private lives of society's victims" (173).

Through this "privatization" of social issues, the "voyeuristic" aspect of the program is introduced. By removing the viewer from context, the guests become visual objects for the distribution of guilt and blame. These aspects directly contribute to the way the problem/solution formula of television talk functions to maintain social hierarchy. Winfrey herself is important for this aspect; she controls the action and is the arbiter of truth and justice.

The third guiding criterion of this chapter involves the viewer's outlook, for which the talk show is presented. The viewer's role as spectator is an important part of talk show entertainment. By watching the program, viewers are allowed into a landscape of personal problems and social issues of the participants. Viewers are placed outside the arena of debate and thus may look on without risk. The *Oprah* program examined here is formed around this "voyeurism" principle, that the viewers be allowed to watch and experience a vicarious release—in this case as an act of blame (173). Voyeuristic pleasure is derived by the audience through the program's focus on the private aspects of guests' feelings—beliefs about Jesus Christ.

Solutions on *Oprah* involve processes whereby one view is given a privileged position while another is relegated to the status of scandalized scapegoat. Victims are produced in order to reaffirm the problem/solution format of commercial entertainment television and, on a deeper level, to alleviate cultural anxieties. The problem/solution formula of the talk show works within a privatized landscape where participants and scene become part of a circus of blame in which the actors fight to affirm their beliefs by putting others down. The physical characteristics of the *Oprah* set, the technology used, and the participants all contribute to this outcome. Viewers are shown three types of actors and the moral arguments they represent. These three include the guests, host, and audience. The guests represent the initial objects of curiosity and interest. Guests are typically placed in the most exposed position and are used to enhance the rhetorical positioning of good versus evil. The audience plays the role of emotional cheerleader for the competing positions and views. It also represents elements of disorder and confusion, and enhances the program's energy.

Winfrey provides the third visual focus of attention. Her image on camera is stabilizing and she is the primary source for identification with viewers. Her physical presence is a daily constant, preceding and succeeding the guests, who appear only once. Winfrey's visual ethos, in many ways, defines the viewer's relationship to audience and guests because her views dominate the line of questioning and direction of the program.

OPRAH WINFREY OFFERS A SOLUTION

Oprah's August 14 show on the *Last Temptation* controversy featured a four-person religious panel that represented opposing Christian views on the film. A fifth guest came in later, toward the end of the program, to reinforce Winfrey's personal view. The program opened with a series of quick clips from the film followed by Winfrey's formative question to guests, audience, and viewers: "Is the film blasphemy or an affirmation of faith?" The question presents the grounds for debate and the problem that was to be solved in the allotted hour. The query offers an either/or response suitable for the format of the program, which would later be dropped for more important issues.

Winfrey framed the debate by introducing her guests and their stances, "You are going to hear from the leaders against the film and from those who support the Christian's right to see this film." Two of her guests approved of the movie and two objected to it. The Rev. Donald Wildmon, United Methodist minister and founder of the American Family Association, and Ted Baehr, editor of *MOVIEGUIDE,* represented the religious conservative position, which opposed the film and its message. "The film says Jesus is a sinner. We think that kind of insensitivity is wrong," commented the Rev. Baehr. The Rev. Wildmon added, "It is a deliberate attack on orthodox Christianity." The two expressed feelings of personal injury and sought public acknowledgement for a violation they believe had occurred. These two occupied the chairs on the left side of the stage in a line of four, all facing front.

On the other side, Charles Bergstrom, consultant for People for the

American Way and a Lutheran minister, and Father John Bannahan, a Roman Catholic priest, represented the religious progressive position, which favored the film's message. These two argued that the film's humanistic message was a valuable tool for public discussion.[2] Both wearing clerical collars, they sought public recognition that religious conservatives had misrepresented them as Christians and Christianity in general. Throughout the program they attacked the two conservatives for what they considered narrow-mindedness and self-serving interests. "It's a tactic by the Christian right. What's troubling is the prejudice creeping into this."

The program proceeded as each guest gave a position statement followed by queries from Winfrey and the audience. A range of issues came up and were debated: the dual nature of Christ, the need for sensitivity to others' religious views, the fact that the two conservatives had not seen the film, freedom of religious expression, lack of tolerance by conservatives, and so forth. From the outset, Winfrey expressed her disapproval of the religious conservative position in various verbal and nonverbal messages. For example, she asked the conservative guests why people should not be allowed to see the film and was unresponsive to their explanations.

Whereas Winfrey's reception of the religious conservative guests was nonresponsive, negative, and challenging, she smiled and nodded when religious progressive guests commented. In this respect her bias influenced how the guests behaved toward one another. For example, Winfrey's affirmative response to religious progressives seemed to allow them the liberty of mocking the conservatives and their comments about the film. Often they could be heard openly laughing at their opponents' responses.

The four religious leaders attacked one another with growing vehemence as the program advanced. Father Bergstrom fired off a rebuttal to Wildmon, who said he was offended by the film. Bergstrom, pointing an accusatory finger, responding, "You don't like it because it shows Jesus as a man." The sincere, perhaps naive, Ted Baehr, who sat next to him, contrasted Father Bannahan's sarcasm toward the religious conservative view. Baehr, arms crossed, pushed to get across his point that the issue was not one of a person's right to see a film, or freedom of interpretation, but of "personal insult" to his religious convictions: "In this film Jesus says I'm a liar. The devil is inside me. Fear is my God."

The debate over theological issues, doctrine, and history were major areas of discussion, especially in the early debate between guests. Major differences in interpretation contributed to the introduction of the audience to the debate. The following section of dialogue captures the tone and content of the interaction. In it, participants try to both repel the opposing view as well as to reconcile it with their own:

Winfrey (sternly responding to Baehr): Is that why you believe it shouldn't be allowed in theaters?

Bergstrom (cuts in): It's a tactic by the Christian right to take advantage of this so they can raise more money.

Wildmon (responding to Winfrey's last statement): That's an incorrect phrasing of the issue! You said we don't want it allowed in theaters . . .

Bergstrom (interrupts Wildmon): It's the prejudice that's troublesome, that has crept in here, anti-Semitism!

Wildmon (looking at Winfrey in an accusatory manner): What you are doing is pitting Christians against one another.

The producers of the talk show to some degree orchestrated these displays of outright conflict. Former guests and audience members have testified about their experience; they were told by the *Oprah* producers before the show to express themselves freely and spontaneously. A guest who appeared on a program featuring dysfunctional families, Wendy Kaminer, revealed the instructions given to her from one of the *Oprah* people. "Just jump in. Don't wait to be called on" (Carpignano 39). Kaminer went on to say that the *Oprah* producers wanted participants and audience members to interrupt one another, display rude behavior, and be unruly (39). The producers, who sought to create emotional intensity and volatility among the participants in order to generate interest among viewers, enhanced the rude behavior in this *Oprah* program. Audiences are hyped up to build energy, excitement, and greater confrontation between views. On the surface the excitement appears to be fun-filled and lighthearted, but underneath there is a formal structure that uses such energy to setup victims for sacrifice—scapegoats.

Winfrey saved her fifth and final guest, Eric Butterworth, author of *Discover the Power Within You,* for the end of the program, as a way to introduce her solution to the religious dilemma. "My next guest says Jesus was a man who discovered his own divinity and taught that this divinity is in all of us." Butterworth avoided Winfrey's query aimed at the other four clergy, taking the high moral ground instead. "I'm not inclined to get involved with religious controversy," he proclaimed. "My thoughts offer an alternative belief." Butterworth's alternative religious

view argued, "It is the Christ within that we must all seek." His univer-
salistic religious solution is important primarily because it endorses the
host's position. Winfrey endorsed his book, saying she had read it several
times and asserting: "The book changed my life."

By adopting Butterworth's "open-minded" view, Winfrey snubbed the
religious conservative stance, and her theological disagreement with
Baehr and Wildmon then became more pronounced. Butterworth became
a vehicle for inserting her personal religious views into the debate and
what becomes the authoritative word on the controversy. Their mutual
endorsement of a common universal principle offered the audience an
alternative to the two positions taken by the guests, one that was inherently tolerant and inclusive. By taking this position Winfrey could also
avoid any problem that would arise had she endorsed either of the two
options to her initial questions. Most important, Butterworth's aphorism
furnished an appropriate rhetorical device by which Winfrey could shift
emphasis away from specific issues about the film and social implications, to a privatized landscape of personal experience, namely subjective
interpretations concerning the film. Once Winfrey presented Butterworth's view, the solution also became obvious. The theological debate
then became more antagonistic and a new contest developed over purely
private issues among guests and audience. The privatization of religious
beliefs placed greater pressure on the guests to resolve their differences
in some form of open demonstration of reconciliation, which actually
never occurred.

DISAGREEING OVER JESUS

Differences of opinion produced by the program are not surprising or
irregular. Nor is it unusual that the *Oprah* program ended with a sense
of indeterminacy. Religion is a highly personal matter that can link or
divide people. Any common ground for religious dialogue is easily rup-
tured through the voicing of different beliefs about the Christ figure by
studio audience members and guests (such as Greek Orthodox, Jewish,
Unitarian, Protestant, Roman Catholic, agnostic, and so on). Even so in
each religious view there is some common reference (Turner, *Dramas*
136). In other words, Jesus is a dominant symbol with manifold structures and narrative history is the unifying and dividing force in the arguments presented on *Oprah*.

The name also evokes interpretations that mix personal belief, feelings,
and metaphysical constructs with the collective belief. In attempts to
reach consensus on *Oprah* the common, or universal symbolic referent,

Jesus, is unable to accommodate the privatized warrants of individuals. Thus the distinctions between views remain the primary activity of the debate over the film on *Oprah.* As a result, those who make claims to the unified reference to Jesus, that which also refers to collective, or social, hierarchy, must be rejected through privatization. Curiously, in this negation there is also a corresponding unification of the dominant view represented as the advocate of tolerance and free expression. Privatization of the Jesus symbol becomes the rhetorical means by which the program sets up the religious guests in general and religious conservatives in particular for blame. Although Winfrey adheres to the position that all private views about Jesus are equal, she does not sanction all views. Indeed, the rhetorical power of the program comes from the fact that certain views are unacceptable and are shunned. The commonly shared aspects of ideas about Jesus give the program its alienating power, certain beliefs about Christ are rejected while others are endorsed (12).

Winfrey's personal disclosure of private information about her deeply personal faith invoked an intensification of the participants' (guests as well as audience members) attachment to their own, often fanatical, opposition to other views (Turner, *Image* 12). Thus the strong emotional expressions and attacks demonstrated on *Oprah* are products of the unifying of polarities in the symbolic object, Jesus, motivated by their attempts to retain an orderly understanding of the symbol's purpose in their lives (247).

Equally important to this issue is the observation that alienation between participants on *Oprah* occurs when there is a unifying of polarities in the symbolic object, Jesus, in order to retain order (social hierarchy). Views about Jesus provided the principle dividing force in the process of scapegoating. The talk show set out to solve a problem concerning conflicted interpretations of the film and in the process validated a particular moral view of the arguments posed, one that embraces the *Last Temptation,* not for its religious message but as an expression of free speech. The two religious conservatives, who evaluated the film through a theological motif, were judged and banished as the talk show's coherent and palpable solution to the conflict.

The most obvious, and probably most comfortable, solution to the issue for viewers is to agree to disagree about the film. Indeed, the program relies on viewer assumptions about difference and the freedom to be different to create its unified appeal to banish the religious conservatives. The viewer is under an assumption that no harm will come to these participants as a result of the judgment derived on the program. Indeed, in a democracy, disagreement is deemed a healthy sign of meaningful and productive cultural activity. But even in the context of this optimistic view, alliances are formed and enemies identified. The conflict surrounding the film reflects such alliances among religious and quasi-religious groups. In the case of *Oprah,* people gather around those with similar views, in opposition to those with whom they disagree producing mandates of inclusion and exclusion. The *Oprah* show demonstrates this point in the mutual alliance developed among participants with similar views and the dissociation from those with whom harmony could not be met.

Of equal merit is the observation that a mutual agreement among participants to disagree collectively holds some significance because it is a socially derived agreement rather than a private one. Winfrey's agreement to disagree with religious conservatives serves to solidify her opposition to them as symbols of the collective negation—producing a pronounced separation from those who do not belong in a tolerant and open-minded society. Being seen as intolerant, bigoted, and narrow-minded, these conservative figures are all the more worthy of sacrifice to the TV audience, the one collectivity to which Winfrey bows.

The privatized landscape of *Oprah* focuses on those religious ideas and issues that can be examined through personal experience. *Oprah* excludes broader social issues in order to achieve a realistic goal for the one-hour program. This exclusion of the larger cultural context can be identified in, and demonstrated through Butterworth's revelation, "Seek the Christ within." His statement is a clarification that all remedies are personal and private. Naturally the problem then becomes focused on the inability of the two conservative Christians to find personal and private harmony within.

Butterworth's statement, "Seek the Christ within," achieves a linguistic separation of the religious issue being debated from its broader cultural context. Anderson identifies this strategy of separation as a deliberate decontextualization, a "therapeutic deciphering of issues whereby distance is created between participants and the historical context" (160). The "therapeutic deciphering of issues" on *Oprah* presents moral problems solely through a subjective or "private" context. When applied to the segment on the *Last Temptation* controversy this privatization of sacred views reduces the social solution to various visible demonstrations of acceptance or rejection of Winfrey's authority. In *Oprah* this therapeutic language of blame helps identify the guilty persons—Wildmon and Baehr. The source of the problem is clarified through demonstrations of particular behavior and attitudes of resistance, which originate in the religious conservative consciousness, namely their personal unwillingness to be corrected. It follows that the religious conservative view is perceived by Winfrey to violate the individual choice of other participants through the perception that they are demanding that others give up something from their private worlds (155). The two are judged for being intolerant by a program and host that subtly lay the blame for the social conflict on them.

On the surface, Winfrey's disarming and nonjudgmental faith is appealing because it does not pose such a threat. Quite the contrary, it assumes a posture of universal acceptance of all views and beliefs. Butterworth's truism appears to embrace tolerance and inclusion. It seems to be thoroughly nonthreatening, open-minded, and reasonable. Nevertheless, to frame the solutions to such age-old religious quarrels in such simplistic terms makes Butterworth's suggestion, "Seek the Christ within," seem trite, bordering on the ridiculous. Yet as a rhetorical device for scapegoating the strategy works quite well. By reducing right and wrong to a simple lack of openness and tolerance on the part of the two religious conservatives, the host likewise reduces them to objects of guilt and blame thus also relieving the audience and viewers of more complex and possibly frightening ideas about the society they inhabit.

PRODUCTION TECHNIQUE AND THE
RHETORIC OF BLAME

Winfrey's rhetorical position and line of questioning are enhanced by the use of these stylistic and compositional elements of the medium. The talk show operates through the camera, the staging, and the choreography, which increase the level of involvement and interaction through conflict. The set layout includes the two main sections, the stage area and audience seating area. Other physical characteristics include camera positions, colors, design features, and so on. These factors contribute to the scapegoating of religious leaders in general and religious conservatives in particular.

Visual structures reinforce the process of ritual alienation through composition, shot selection, and editing. Cameras pick up the action, rotating from guest, to host, then to audience reaction. Individual shots maintain a concentration on a respondent with intermittent cutaways to capture the audience's reactions. There is no major imbalance in the way the guests were presented, but the program does have a repeated pattern of shots that supports the rhetorical position of the host.

In the first shot of the sequence Winfrey asks one of the religious conservatives a question. A close-up of the respondent follows this shot with a cutaway inserted. The cutaway shows an audience member who is expressing disapproval facially. The cutaway is followed by a return to the respondent, who is physically leaning forward in an attempt to convince the host and audience of his argument (pleading position). The shot is followed by a return to Winfrey who then asks a religious progressive on the stage to respond. The final shot includes this respondent rebutting the religious conservative. Music comes up under to indicate a coming break. This sequence of shots conveys a sense of insecurity on the part of the religious conservative guests, particularly in Rev. Wildmon. The camera work enhances the stature of the religious progressives through visual and verbal affirmation from the host.

Scapegoating activity is enhanced by the way the camera captures the movement and reaction of all the guests, presenting them in an unfavorable light. Their views on the matter are sensationalized and scandalized by the intense visual focus of the camera on their every gesture and word. The more anxious, emotional, and uncomfortable a guest becomes, the greater is the camera's interest. In this way viewers are presented with an exciting visual conflict as they look into the private worlds of the Christian clergymen to watch them spit nasty comments at each other.

The underlying problem of the *Last Temptation* for Winfrey is the issue of free choice; people should have the right to see the film. As host and principle authority for the audience she pursues a line of questioning constantly going back to this issue when engaging religious conservatives. Even when religious conservatives responded with, "Yes, others did have a right to see the film," Winfrey acted as if they had said "No." Her physical affect, facial expression, and gestures portray disapproval and disdain for their views.

By following a line of questioning that repeatedly returned to issues of free speech, Winfrey reinforced the conclusion that the two religious conservatives were trying to censor the film. The two other clergy on the stage helped make this point stick with various comments linking religious conservative guests to stereotypes: televangelism, greed, censors, and even anti-Semitism. The religious conservative guests concentrated primarily on personal issues over the film's content and personal feelings, while Winfrey continued to question them about issues of free speech. The contrast present in these two strains of argument is important for how *Oprah* eventually set up the Christian religious guests as scapegoats of daytime talk.

The development and strengthening of Oprah's polemic against the conservatives reached their peak when Butterworth came on stage with his profound insight about the "Christ within." Religious conservatives were then faced with an ultimatum: to demonstrate openness and tolerance or become objects of disgust—the defining moment whereby the viewers, through Winfrey, pronounce judgment on the two religious conservatives. By this time the talk show had placed the religious conservatives in the untenable position of sacrificing their personal convictions in order to comply with the Butterworth maxim and Winfrey's remedy. Such a sacrifice would not, however, reverse the flow of blame because the victims have already been labeled and objectified. Their membership in the world of *Oprah* has been contaminated in part because of their religious views, but, more important, because they have been selected and set apart to be scapegoats regardless of the legitimacy of their claims.

Given these revelations it is no surprise to find that the program closed in confusion, discouragement, ridicule of others' views, and greater defensiveness between participants. Such defensiveness and distance are a common product of talk shows, leading one to conclude that the problem/solution formula as demonstrated in *Oprah* is one of "repressive tolerance" (Marcuse 164). It is argued here that in a capitalistic framework of commercial television, tolerance is used as a means of repressing marginals (164). Likewise, as has been demonstrated here, the *Oprah* show, as a mass-mediated format, provides significant insight about how repressive tolerance can be translated into forms of scapegoating.

There are many ways to examine the *Oprah* program that could derive other results. Indeed, one could see in it many healthy developments. People were debating religion and religious belief in a nationally televised forum. Such disclosure does have value in a democratic society. Nevertheless, talk shows and their hosts always argue for openness and free speech from a privileged position.

CONCLUDING REMARKS

The *Oprah* show is an arena, a microsystem of the *Last Temptation* conflict in which a problem is presented, discussion advanced, and a solution produced. The outcome, as has been demonstrated here, reveals enhanced boundaries between social segments and incremental progress in a process of blame. As this examination has demonstrated, privatization and voyeurism are primary vehicles for scapegoating in the daytime talk show.

The process of scapegoating, as it takes place on the *Oprah* show, is significant for the way it reveals human characteristics and mass-mediated communication processes as they are connected to ritual functions of contemporary society and to the general perpetuation of a scapegoat model through a commercial production formula. In this sense, the show fortifies a social hierarchy (the entertainment industry) and its moral imperatives by providing audiences with enemies to dislike and despise. It does this by privatizing social issues and by presenting the private world of its guests to audiences as an object of voyeuristic pleasure. Beyond the happy, positive world of daytime talk is a culture that is increasingly reliant on the commercial formula of scapegoating to provide vicarious empowerment, ways for people to ritually to overcome the complexities and tensions of contemporary American society. We may say that, as these tensions increase, so increases our need for scapegoats innocently presented to us through programs such as *Oprah.*

Scapegoating is a voyeuristic pleasure that encourages viewers to attack the humanity of those with whom they disagree. Broadly speaking, experiencing the humiliation of others is a common human means of separating from one's own sense of humiliation, be it religious, economic, educational, race based, or other form of evil. The scapegoat victims (religious conservative guests) allow viewers to separate from their own failings, and narrow their range of accountability (Miller 165). Viewers project their failure to be tolerant and open-minded onto the Rev.s Wildmon and Baehr and cast them into a media nonexistence.[3] The purveyors of blame, talk show audiences, succeed in reclassifying the religious conservative guests, as less than human by labeling them "fundamentalists." *Oprah* scapegoats these guests by denying any consideration of their views and humiliates them by virtue of this denial (Miller 280). In this way of thinking it is understandable that commercial television talk shows would present people in increasingly degrading ways—the *Jerry Springer Show.*

NOTES

1. The *Los Angeles Times,* for example, concentrated on various aspects of the protest, particularly local protest activity. The *New York Times* followed a similar pattern with emphasis on developments surrounding the film's release and reception. The distribution of stories for both the *Los Angeles Times* and the *New York Times* is concentrated in August 1988. Of the 13 days when stories were printed in each, eight were in August. Coverage in the *Daily Variety* was slightly less concentrated. On the 12 dates when stories were printed, only five were in August.

2. Bergstrom and Bannahan attended the July 12 screening for clergy in New York. Neither Rev. Wildmon or Rev. Baehr had seen the film.

3. It is worth noting that these disenfranchised religious conservatives to this day have not resolved their disputes over the film's meaning through media forums such as *Oprah,* or through any other corrective media debate. The majority of the parties who represent religious conservatives maintain their claims of hurt and humiliation, rigidly defending their sacred religious beliefs.

Chapter 7

SCAPEGOATING AS LEGAL PROCESS

Religious conservatives sought to uphold and maintain a set of religious principles in an attempt to keep the film out of their communities. Failing this mission, some religious conservatives sought satisfaction in the courts and through the implementation of legal edicts. Here the moral code of the church confronted the legal code of the American justice system in failed endeavors to make the studio comply. The examination of these efforts generally reinforces the view that the courts apply a form of linguistic scapegoating in order to ensure their authority and autonomy. The moral claims introduced by religious conservatives are thus denied legitimacy.

This chapter concentrates on three failed efforts to ban the *Last Temptation* from local communities. The Nayak and Greb cases are important because each went to circuit court, then to district court, and, finally, to the Supreme Court, where rulings were handed down and sustained. A third case, the Rev. Rowe's invocation of an outdated Massachusetts blasphemy law, is helpful for putting the religious argument in context.

The analysis follows a narrow focus, relating the law to moral claims about the *Last Temptation* in order to find out how the rulings contribute the activity of scapegoating. Legal recourse is examined as part of the final element of the process of scapegoating in which the legal system sanctions a newly aligned relationship between liberal progressive and religious conservative movements. The power affixed to these rulings has important implications for how the *Last Temptation* succeeded as a form of free speech and as a distinct religious document. The assertion forwarded here is that these legal rulings unify the law in a process of linguistic purification where all forms of opposition to the film's exhibition, including religion and its moral codes, are defeated (Fish 142). The scapegoating process completes its cycle in legal rulings, which solidify social relations in formal oppositions. Through the law, the ritual object of defamation (religious language) is reincorporated into the language structures of society and its various social hierarchies in more abstract form.

This chapter argues that the courts not only employed and applied moral components to the *Last Temptation* cases, but they also introduced the process of scapegoating into their decisions concerning the film. In line with this orientation, the legal code is treated as what Burke refers to as an "agonistic instrument" (*Grammar* 357). Its language and mandates describe a condition of opposition to certain forces, which threaten its authority and autonomy. As Burke puts it, "The purpose is to establish some motivational fixity on opposition to something thought liable to endanger its fixity" (357). In the case of the *Last Temptation,* religion is the enemy of the law, implicitly as a threat to its autonomy and unity, and explicitly as a threat to its linguistic forms.

RELIGION AS AN ENEMY OF THE LAW

Each of the religious conservative complaints launched against Universal has a different context and situation yet maintains elements in common with the others. Each views the law as a tool for moral sanctions; each places law below the religious moral code; each relies on local elements to substantiate claims; each views the law as an enforcement tool for the moral code.

Three people brought a complaint against Universal and Cineplex Odeon Films in the Pittsburgh District Court. The three, referred to as Greb, argued that the film was offensive to their religious views. They sought to bar its distribution, or to force changes in its title and script to omit all references to Jesus ("U.S. Supreme Court" 1). Greb presented the following argument as to why the *certiorari* should be granted:

Because this case represents a collision between the First Amendment free exercise clause of religion and the freedom of speech clause—a collision which has produced violence and mass protests, and because of the impact on society, *certiorari* should be granted to better define the area of protected speech (particularly since similar speech was protected when directed against a racial group) in a situation where one's God and one's religion is subjected to ridicule, mockery and harassment through the media of a movie. ("U.S. Supreme Court" 1)

Greb's argument emphasizes the contradictions present in the First Amendment. The successful reincorporation of the religious moral code into the law is, to some extent, premised on how religion is interpreted in light of the freedom of speech clause. Correspondingly, the argument relies on the vagueness of the free speech clause to argue that such speech, as is found in the content of the *Last Temptation,* should not be protected. The assertion asks for clarification of "protected speech" and assumes that some speech is harmful to the public.

The Pittsburgh District of the Pennsylvania Superior Court threw out the suit in October 1988. The decision was appealed and upheld by a state appellate court ("U.S. Supreme Court" 2). It was then appealed to the Supreme Court, which refused to bar the showing of the film ("Religion" 1). Without comment the nation's highest court let stand the ruling that the film is protected free speech ("U.S. Supreme Court" 2). That ruling reads, "*The Last Temptation of Christ* is, per se, entitled to unlimited and absolute protection under the First Amendment without any consideration being given to its content" (2).

The court ruled against Greb based on the "relative constitutionality" of the freedom of speech clause of the First Amendment (*Grammar* 386).[1] By taking this position, the court denied any relationship between the law and moral concerns, both in terms of the religious nature of the film and in terms of its specific content (*States Law* 90). The ruling is consistent with the idea that in order to insure the relevance of the law for future generations; the ruling must subordinate all moral claims to generalized and abstract meaning (*Grammar* 365). The Constitution's provisions are adapted to the concrete conditions presented in the complaint as a means of denying their legitimacy at the local level (366).[2]

In the Greb case the law enhances its scope and expands its authority by eliminating competing language and ideas, thus also maintaining its uniformity and autonomy. By its very absence, religious language is repelled from forensic discourse and action. As Stanley Fish points out, law is in the business of producing the authority it invokes. "It establishes its independence from the very social and political values that are its content. It maintains itself by differentiation and by exclusion of the discourse that surrounds it" (111). For the court to have responded affirmatively to Greb's moral argument would have required that it limit its authority and localize its scope. Fish observes, "Morality would make laws which would lack its most salient qualities—generality and stability" (142). The law maintains its purity and fixity in examples such as the Greb ruling.[3]

In a second lawsuit, Veda Nayak of Houston objected to the distribution of the film, claiming it was a "defamatory interpretation" of the life of Jesus Christ that infringed on the plaintiff's, and other believers', constitutional right of freedom of worship and religion ("U.S. Supreme Court" 1). The Nayak complaint posed two valuable questions regarding the contemporary tension between free speech and religious beliefs and the role of legal interpretation in reestablishing balance and order:

> 1) Can defendants claim constitutional privilege of protected speech for their alleged profanity, obscenity, and defamatory falsehood regarding Christ in their film? (2) In multi-religious/racial society, can a religious group, using mass media, insult religious beliefs of another group, and claim shelter under First Amendment? ("U.S. Supreme Court" 1)

The Fifth Circuit Court of Appeals ruled in the Nayak case that the "Trial of religious issues raised by the plaintiff would violate the First Amendment" ("U.S. Supreme Court" 1). The U.S. Supreme Court, in its decision to uphold the lower court ruling, added:

> Freedom of thought, which includes freedom of religious beliefs, is basic in a society of free men. It embraces the right to maintain theories of life and of death and of the hereafter which are rank heresies to followers of the orthodox faiths. Heresy trials are foreign to our Constitution. ("Fifth Circuit Dismisses" 1)

This reading allows the high court to promote a set of generalized principles, rights, and duties as a "grand promissory unity" that sets itself against the religious concept proposed by Nayak (Burke, *Grammar* 349). Likewise, it radically privatizes morality and religious belief. The wording "religious belief" is subordinate to "freedom of thought" which underlies "freedom of speech" in a linguistic hierarchy. The use of the term "foreign" is pivotal in placing morality and religious conservative arguments at the bottom of this hierarchy. The Constitution is above heresy; it alienates any form of reference to such activity in a process of ritual cleansing.

The ruling used the word "freedom" to cover a full range of human experiences that are generalized here in two phrases, "freedom of thought" and "freedom of religious belief," which, combined, equal "a free society."[4] The first and most important element in this series of thoughts is found in the phrase, "freedom of thought," which alludes to a stable relationship between the individual and society. A free society is premised on freedom of thought and the two complement one another in a socially balanced environment ("Fifth Circuit Court Dismisses" 1). The protection of "freedom of speech" does not function primarily as an act of will or religious expression; it acts as a negative sanction against what it is not—"bondage" (Burke, *Grammar* 334). The moral code of the Christian church is viewed as a binding and limiting instrument.

Scorsese's transgression is of significance simply because the medium through which violation is registered involves a mass-mediated technology brought from another context. The *Last Temptation,* as a transgressive act, is more threatening than say an offensive image placed in a store window, and much more difficult to correct. One may interpret this to say that the medium of film may have contributed to the court decisions. Because of the nonspecificity of the offensive object, celluloid, the violation itself becomes an abstraction. One of the liberal progressive rebuttals to conservative complaints demonstrates this point: "It's only a movie."

Scorsese's film, as a religious opinion, had efficacy in the broader social arena because it was presented as a nationally distributed movie. It thus had power to disrupt the social harmony in a wide range of individual communities while also providing the courts an opportunity to unify and purify the law. The legal cases against the film gave the courts good reasons to extend their reach and control over religious discourse itself. As a protected representation of free speech, the *Last Temptation* serves to sanction the persecution and victimization of religious conservatives.

RECODIFYING BLASPHEMY

Law and legal discourse have not always been clearly separated from moral dictums. Changes in the language of the law occur over a long period of time. Indeed, one can look back and find statutes that link moral and legal elements. An outdated blasphemy law provides more clues as to how scapegoating functions in the rulings discussed here. A pastor in Springfield, Massachusetts, considered filing a lawsuit against a local theater, citing the state's nineteenth-century blasphemy law as his defense (Bazinet 2). The Rev. Curtis Rowe said, "You know there is a blasphemy law in Massachusetts, we have asked police to enforce the law [*sic*], which is very clearly being broken by the film" (Bazinet 2). Rowe's reference to the outdated blasphemy law creates a vivid image of the religious conservative's view of the relationship between law and religion in contemporary society. His argument never went to court. Rowe dropped the suit on the advice of his attorney, who suggested that the law could not be enforced.[5]

The nineteenth-century blasphemy law reflects a distinctively Christian view in a set of moral commands that strike directly at the communication between God and creature. The Massachusetts statute is quoted here in full:

Blasphemy: Whoever willfully blasphemes the holy name of God by denying, cursing or contumeliously reproaching God, his creation, government or final judging of the world, or by cursing or contumeliously reproaching Jesus Christ or the Holy Ghost, or by cursing or contumeliously reproaching or exposing to contempt and ridicule, the holy word of God contained in the holy scriptures shall be punished by imprisonment in jail for not more than one year or by a fine of not more than three hundred dollars, and may also be bound to good behavior. ("Annotated Laws" C272)

This law derives its meaning from religious principles, which uniformly reinforce a theological premise that is foreign to contemporary legal discourse. It sews historical antecedents to the vertical order of things, making secular law coterminous with Christian religious hierarchies; moral and legal language meet in the mutual sanctioning of the other (Burke, *Grammar* 343).

The fact that the Massachusetts law could not be enforced reflects a broader evolutionary process that, over a 200-year period, has separated religion from law. Burke writes, "The theocratic association was gradually dissociated with faith and knowledge changing their relationship, step by step, from that of contemporary counterparts to antagonist counterparts" (343). This explains, in part, the disparity that exists between current legal rulings on the *Last Temptation* and Rowe's assumptions concerning its moral elements. The language of the Massachusetts law is charged with moral content that is foreign to current legal process and code.

One explanation for the disparity between this outdated law and the court rulings is provided by Fish who points out, "Morality frustrates the law because recourse to morality will always be recourse to someone, or some group's challengeable moral vision" (142). Fish further clarifies, "The law does not wish to be absorbed by or declared subordinate to some other not legal structure of concern" (143).

The separation of law from moral code seems valid until one recognizes that the Massachusetts blasphemy statute is also a legal statue that was once applied. Even though it can no longer be enforced, it still embodies the formal properties of law and legal discourse. In this sense, the First Amendment, while it conflicts with the moral code in these complaints, actually has the same formal characteristics as the blasphemy statute. It is a negative sanction designed to endorse one type of speech to the exclusion of another. In the rhetoric of scapegoating, the First Amendment serves the same function as the blasphemy law—to unify and purify its identity in a dialectic opposition to the sacrificial object (*Grammar* 407). The Greb and Nayak rulings follow the same principle function as the blasphemy law but at a much more abstract level.[6] Blasphemy remains as the formal object of persecution but the process of scapegoating is hidden by legal discourse.

In making this shift in emphasis from content to form, one can see that it is the process of ritual alienation that remains a constant element in legal rulings through the decontextualization of language. At this juncture between the language of an abstract law and a concrete moral code of an antiquated blasphemy statute the rhetoric of scapegoating is precisely devised and recognizable. The law does not, as Fish argues, escape morality but actually reinforces it because, ultimately, the law's abstract existence is rooted in some historical context. It operates as a moral code to someone, at some time.

CONCLUDING REMARKS

Instead of removing religious components, the Greb and Nayak rulings actually reintroduce the scapegoating process into the law. Thus, when the Supreme Court ruled that it has nothing to do with heresy charges, it was exercising its moral authority in an act of ritual alienation, re-inserting the scapegoat process into American legal discourse. In these rulings the courts were both affirming the law's formal existence while denying their own moral qualities, distancing its own moral language from that of the Christian religion. In this way the rulings cleansed the law of any moral language and the discourse of its religious antecedents, while reimplementing a moral process, scapegoating, in its language.

One could say that the law's formal existence is dependent on the success with which it implements the scapegoat process. To put it another way, the law's authority, in the case of the *Last Temptation,* depends on acts of personal interpretation of religious free-speech expressions that are rhetorical in nature. So, even though the law as a document is abstract, its application here is concrete. The law is, to put it literally, an extension of Universal Studios' act of victimization.

The rulings examined here represent incremental steps of ritual dissociation of religion from secular social order both in terms of legal rulings and mandates. The rulings concerning the *Last Temptation* provide evidence that the legal code and religious moral code have become increasingly incompatible.

In these rulings, there is a "motivational fixity" exercised by the courts in opposition to threats to their authority. The courts unified the law's position against moral claims of religious conservatives. In this sense, the Greb and Nayak decisions represent a new principle or merger. This merger does not so much involve the separation of law from moral code as it involves the production of new forms of purified language that carefully conceal the object of blame. In this way the law maintains its authority and autonomy as the dialectic opposite to moral claims, particularly those presented by religious conservatives concerning *The Last Temptation of Christ.*

NOTES

1. Writing in the 1950s, Burke distinguishes two constitutional theories. A "Strict constructionist" picks some clause and judges a measure by reference to it—the essentializing approach (380). The "broad constructionist" tests the measure by reference to all the wishes of the Constitution rationalizing its decision by rule of the majority. This "proportional" strategy requires hierarchies among "disjunctive wishes," meaning some wishes are more important than others (382).

2. The application here seeks primarily to clarify how the courts came to a particular interpretation that "disallowed" religious concerns and legal redress, and the cultural implications of such action for future challenges.

3. Because of the Constitution's "motivational fixity," its universal and ineffable quality, persons like Denby, Corliss, and Valenti could promote their position in support of freedom of speech "while enjoying maximum freedom of argument" (*Grammar* 360). They confronted the un-free "fundamentalists" with the virtues of "free men" in the broadest sense.

4. The idea of "free men," says Burke, "can lead back to the heavenly or Edenic origins," although these origins are eliminated from the companion term "men" (387). "Free men" is oxymoronic. This becomes clearer if we simply stop to realize that the very basis of the notion of a man/person involves all

kinds of utilitarian elements concerning survival. A free "man," theoretically, is one who is able to survive in the context of a competitive world. In addition, "free men" are those who have the economic power to act out their wishes. Thus freedom cannot be synonymous with an ontological state of "being."

5. Three years later, the Massachusetts legislature would take up the cause with a bill against any art that satirizes religious figures, with similar effect *(Seattle Times* A3).

6. The pragmatic angle taken here serves only the purpose of bringing to the surface important elements about the relationship between scapegoating and legal actions. It does not make claims about formalism, pragmatism, or other orientations toward law and legal theory.

Chapter 8

CONCLUSION

The *Last Temptation* controversy was an episode, a cultural performance, where proponents of two competing views, religious conservative and liberal progressive, met to debate a religious film and to challenge one another. In this contest, the domain of popular film became a battleground where interpretive communities came to solidify their positions and alignments to one another through processes of scapegoating. The enlightened and hoped for results of the affair would be increased dialogue or some other indication that progress has been made toward a common ideal—a more tolerant society. This study supports the contrary outcome, that the deep social upheaval generated by the *Last Temptation* controversy produced greater cultural alienation as a result of scapegoating.

The presence of scapegoating found in the affair demonstrates that a strong degree of intolerance exists between two primary segments of American society. Indeed, the debate over the *Last Temptation*, in many ways, lacked those qualities we so readily identify with a tolerant people. In a process of scapegoating, these competing moral discourses generated and reinforced antipathy toward one another that remains today.

Scapegoating, as a process of linguistic transformation and cultural purgation, points to deeply seated anxieties within religious conservative and liberal progressive factions and to the most significant aspects of identity formation and belonging. The arguments over the film developed as a direct result of these pressures and as a result of hierarchical uncertainty. Scapegoating provides a map of the changes in these social configurations and, to some degree, is helpful in evaluating the role of religious language in sustaining and reproducing arguments.

At one level, the texts studied exemplify a civility between parties in which potential for alleviation of tension was possible. At some point those linguistic indicators of reconciliation were reduced or eliminated, discarded for a more direct language of retribution and blame. Scorsese and Universal Studios proceeded to make the film in the face of enormous resistance, all the time denying it was a form of provocation. The art film became headline news during the summer of 1988 when millions of religious conservatives rallied behind the cry of blasphemy. The religious protest, the largest ever launched against a film, was fueled by mass-mediated communication and religious broadcasters who spread the language of victimization. As a strategy for reestablishing order and harmony between secular and religious domains and their representative hierarchies, the organized effort to stop the film's production and release advanced ideas that the entertainment industry and Universal Studios are immoral and exploitive groups. The distinctively religious cry of blasphemy was somewhat predictable and plain to the eye; it was no surprise to see the process of scapegoating manifest itself in the language and arguments put forth by this segment. The intent and nature of the organized protest played heavily on moral concerns and the film's treatment of their most sacred figure.

Scorsese's fully human Jesus, a demystified and highly subjectivized Christ, radically altered the traditional function of the sacrificial victim as well as the formal relations between good and evil. In his psychological battle to resolve this tension, it is never clear whether God and the Devil are part of Jesus' conscience or external forces representing universal religious principles. The film, while it was interpreted in various ways, represents a transgressive text, a provocation that unleashed the forces of scapegoating. In it are the offensive components that produced a wide-scale debate and activated mechanisms of alienation. Confirming the religious conservative complaints, this study observes that the offensive elements of the film could not have been accidental.

In response to the national protest against the film, Universal and its supporters were defiant. Polarized by the perceived threat of censorship, liberal progressives unified in a defense of freedom of speech. These voices solidified their resistance to, and dislike for, religious conservatives through their own rituals of blame. Scapegoating provided a means of reestablishing secure boundaries with religious conservative forces in society and would alleviate societal guilt produced by the failings of a social paradigm.

At its peak, the affair attracted the attention of news media, film critics and reviewers, commentators, talk shows, news magazines, and a broad range of cultural groups and segments. Many of these voices converged to battle with religious conservatives over fundamental rights and religious principles. Film reviewers and critics lashed out at religious conservatives in highly inflammatory and emotional language that, in many ways, mirrored those statements of their religious archenemy. At times Universal's defenders resorted to distinctively religious ideas and language to defend the film, often applying strategies used by religious conservatives to produce counterclaims about the film's religious meaning and significance. Certain distinctions that separate liberal progressives from the "fundamentalist" Christians fell away. Mainstream reviewers and critics around the country were talking about the film as if it was a testimony to their personal faith in God. The common failure among these voices to see and acknowledge the contradictions present in such arguments bears testimony to the enduring power and ubiquity of scapegoating as a means of social correction.

Liberal progressives demonstrated no awareness that they were persecuting anyone; they were simply defending the sacred mandates of the Constitution and First Amendment. To these defenders the film's legitimacy as a work of art and as protected speech was indisputable. They set it outside the realm of cultural dispute even as they used it to blame religious conservatives for all forms of social ills. The intolerance and narrow-mindedness present in the film went unrecognized because its defenders had so effectively decontextualized the religious rhetoric of scapegoating. Correspondingly, the *Last Temptation* was effective as a document of blame because its rhetorical meanings were so well rationalized and hidden by the film's creators as well as its intellectual defenders. They were caught up in the logic of their representation of the film, believing in the guilt of their adversaries (Girard 40). Indeed, thousands of pages of reviews, biographies, and analysis assumed that the arguments made in defense of the film were reasoned and sound.

In other arenas of debate, such as television talk shows and the courts, the efficacy of scapegoating as a mode of social control was confirmed. The same language of blame found in letters, releases, and statements of both positions can be found in the content of the *Oprah* episode studied here. *Oprah*'s segment on the *Last Temptation* supports the assertion that such rituals of blame are perpetuated in popular culture discourse, content and form. *Oprah* operates as a television arena of scapegoating by producing an environment where the ritual subject of blame may be extricated from legitimate involvement in the debate. In this privatized landscape audiences are positioned as voyeurs who judge good and evil according to *Oprah*'s presentation of the problem and are offered simplistic solutions that tend to affirm the program's own claims.

The court actions discussed in this study demonstrate how secular law and religious claims to power within the culture became polarized in opposition to the fundamental premises of the other. One result of this polarization is the nullification of the religious conservative agenda in influencing the content of secular law. The most significant finding in this regard involves the observation that the courts, although denying all religious reference in the specific language content, reproduced new and more advanced processes of blame in the language of their rulings. The failure of legal attempts to stop the film's exhibition, on the part of religious conservatives, indicates that their agenda, as a moral guide for American society, has lost much of its relevance and application. The courts treat the arguments over the film with indifference, refusing to consider religious factors in their rulings.

These observations lead to the realization that the long accepted boundaries between religious and secular language are collapsing even as the social hierarchies become separated into distinct and exclusive realms of governance. This assertion conflicts with the idea that American society is actually becoming more secularized and less religious. If this were true, then why do these ancient processes continue to play a central role in cultural transformations? It seems more plausible to say that America is becoming more secular only in the sense that these traditional religious elements have been decontextualized and gradually separated from their original religious forms and symbols. There is no indication that the secular culture has surpassed or evolved beyond the religious processes of blame identified as scapegoating.

Of equal concern is the fact that the intellectual machinery of our secularized culture has no apparent instrument for controlling such processes of scapegoating. Without such protective instruments, cultural scapegoating will gradually reduce the institutionalized ideals of a tolerant, democratic society to self-justifying modes of persecution and blame, carrying us backward to more primitive social configurations.

As an indicator of historical trends, the *Last Temptation* controversy demonstrates the lasting power of scapegoating on our communication processes. This enduring marker of our religious past continues to shape the cultural landscape of America and will likely play a major role in future developments. Even though we cannot extricate it from our social hierarchies, and their communication, an increased awareness of its influence may prompt a renewed commitment to processes of dialogue and reconciliation. An elevated awareness of the destructive effects of scapegoating tends to level the playing field and democratize the debate, opening the way for honest and constructive dialogue between competing segments.

SELECTED BIBLIOGRAPHY

"Action Seeking to Bar Distribution of the Film 'The Last Temptation of Christ' Are Dismissed." *Entertainment Law Reporter* 12.11 (1991).

American Society for the Defense of Tradition, Family, and Property (ASDTFP). Advertisement. *New York Times* 12 Aug. 1988: A7.

Anderson, Robin. *Consumer Culture & TV Programming.* Boulder, CO: Westview Press, 1995.

Angelica, Mother M. Letter to Bishop Howard J. Hubbard D.D. 21 July 1988.

Ansen, David, and Andrew Nurr. "The Arts: Movies, Wrestling with 'Temptation'." *Newsweek* 15 Aug. 1988: 56–57.

"Archbishop Calls for Protest of Film." *The Catholic Advocate* 3 Aug. 1988: 5.

"Archbishop's Statement." *The Catholic Advocate* 3 Aug. 1988: 5.

Babbington, Bruce, and Peter W. Evans. *Biblical Epics: Sacred Narratives in the Hollywood Cinema.* Manchester: Manchester University Press, 1993.

Baehr, Ted. Editorial. *MOVIEGUIDE* 18 July 1988: 11.

Bal, Mieke. "Experiencing Murder: Ritualistic Interpretation of Ancient Texts." *Victor Turner and the Construction of Cultural Criticism.* Ed. Kathleen M. Ashley. Indianapolis: Indiana University Press, 1990. 3–30.

Barrett, Mary Ellin. "Scorsese's 'Temptation': Not Exactly by the Book." *USA Today* 12 July 1988: D6.

Bazinet, Kenneth R. "Fundamentalists Put Film Suit on Hold." *United Press International* [New York] 8 Sept. 1988, BC cycle.

Beehler, Don. Letter to John Smale. 1 Nov. 1988.

Benson, Sheila. Review of *The Last Temptation of Christ,* by Martin Scorsese. *Los Angeles Times* 12 Aug. 1988: sec. 6: 1.

Billy Graham Ministries. Press Release. 18 July 1988.

Bird, Brian. "Film Protesters Vow Long War on Universal." *Christianity Today* 16 Sept. 1988: 41–43.

Biskind, Peter, and Susan Linfield. "Chalk Talk." *American Film* Nov. 1986: 30–34.

Blake, R. A. "An Autopsy of 'Temptation'." *America* 4 Mar. 1989: 199–201.

———. "Redeemed in Blood: The Sacramental Universe of Martin Scorsese." *The Journal of Popular Film & Television* 24.1 Spring 1996: 2–9.

———. "The Universal Christ." *America* 27 Aug. 1988: 99–102.

Bliss, Michael. *The Word Made Flesh: Catholicism & Conflict in the Films of Martin Scorsese.* London: Scarecrow Press, 1995.

Blowen, Michael. " 'Temptation' Sneaks into Stores." *The Boston Globe* 30 June 1989: 43.

Boyar, Jay. "Three Visionaries Direct the Decade." *Orlando Sentinel Tribune* 25 Nov. 1990: F1.

Bravin, Jess. "Hundreds at Mall Protest Screening of 'Temptation'." *Los Angeles Times* 20 Aug. 1988: Pt. 2: 1.

———. " 'Temptation' to Open in Santa Ana on Friday." *Los Angeles Times* 18 Aug. 1988: sec. 6: 10.

Braxton, Greg. "'The Last Temptation of Christ'; Scorsese Ends Long Quest to Make Kazantzakis Novel." *Los Angeles Times* 12 Aug. 1988: sec. 6: 1.

———. "200 Christians Protest Universal's Depiction of Jesus." *Los Angeles Times* 17 July 1988: sec. 2: 4.

Broeske, Pat H. "'The Last Temptation of Christ'; Scorsese Ends Long Quest to Film Kazantzakis' Novel." 12 Aug. 1988: Calendar, sec. 6: 1. *Infotrac: National Newspaper Index.* CD-ROM. Information Access. Oct. 1993.

———. "Universal Asked to 'Destroy' Scorsese's Film About Christ." *Los Angeles Times* 13 July 1988: Calendar, sec. 6: 1.

Bruning, Fred. "A Thorny Debate for the Faithful." *Maclean's* 5 Sept. 1988: 9.

Buchanan, Patrick. Editorial. *Glendale News Press* 27 July 1988: A9.

Buckley, William F. "That's Entertainment!" *National Review* 2 Sept. 1988: 17.

Burke, Kenneth. *Attitudes toward History.* Berkeley: U of California P, 1937.

———. *Counter-Statement.* New York: Harcourt, Brace, & Company, 1953.

———. "A Dramatistic View of the Origins of Language." *Quarterly Journal of Speech* 38 (1952): 251–64.

———. *A Grammar of Motives.* Berkeley: U of California P, 1969.

———. "Linguistic Approaches to Problems of Education." *Yearbook of the National Society for the Study of Education.* Ed. Nelson Henry. Chicago: U of Chicago P, 1955. sec. I: 259–303.

———. *Perspectives by Incongruity.* Bloomington: Indiana UP, 1964.

———. *A Rhetoric of Motives.* New York: Braziller Inc., 1955.

———. *The Rhetoric of Religion.* Boston: Beacon Press, 1961.

Byrge, Duane. "Last Temptation of Christ." *The Hollywood Reporter* 8 Aug. 1988: 8.

Canby, Vincent. "In the Theaters, An American Harvest." Review of *The Last*

Temptation of Christ, by Martin Scorsese. *New York Times* 25 Sept. 1988: 23.

Caprignano, Paolo, Robin Anderson, Stanley Arowitz, and William Difazio. "Chatter in the Age of Electronic Reproduction: TV Talkshows and the Public Mind." *Social Text* Summer/Fall 1992: 33–35.

Carter, C. Allen. *Kenneth Burke and the Scapegoat Process.* Norman: U of Oklahoma P, 1996.

Carter, Stephen L. *Culture of Disbelief.* New York: Anchor Books, 1993.

Caruth, Cathy. "Traumatic Awakenings." *Performity and Performance.* Ed. Andrew Parker. New York: Routledge, 1994. 89.

"Catholic Bishop Stops Showing of Controversial Film." UPI California 25 Oct. 1989, BC cycle.

Champlin, Charles. "Scorsese in Wake of 'Temptation'." *Los Angeles Times* 19 Jan. 1989: sec. 6: 1.

Chandler, Russell. "25,000 Protest Temptation." *Los Angeles Times* 12 August 1988: sec. 1: 3.

Chanko, Kenneth. "For Dafoe, Playing Christ was a Risk But No Gamble." *Chicago Tribune* 14 Aug. 1988: Arts 6.

———. Review of *The Last Temptation of Christ,* by Martin Scorsese. *Films in Review.* Nov. 1988: 550.

Churnin, Nancy. "Director Says Protests Didn't Close 'Red Noses'." *Los Angeles Times* 9 Sept. 1988: sec. 6: 2.

Clarke, Ronald. "Dustin Hoffman and 'Rain Man' The Oscar Favorites." *Reuter's Library Report* 21 Mar. 1989: 1.

Clements, Marcelle. "Martin Scorsese Has Learned the Hard Way; to Work with Hollywood to Make His Films." *New York Newsday* 10 Nov. 1991: 6.

Collum, Danny D. "Ancient Scandal and Modern Heresy." *Sojourners* Nov. 1988: 37–38.

Colson, Charles. "Weekly Audio Magazine: 'Last Temptation of Christ'." *Focus on the Family* WVCS, Chicago. 12 Nov. 1988.

Cong. Rec. (134.120) 11 Aug. 1988: H6969–6970.

———. (134.120) 13 Oct. 1988: E3433–E3435.

Connelly, Marie Katheryn. *The Films of Martin Scorsese: A Critical Study.* Diss. Case Western Reserve University, 1991. Ann Arbor: UMI, 1991.

Cook, Pam. Review, "The Last Temptation of Christ." *Monthly Film Bulletin* Oct. 1988: 287.

Corliss, Richard. "Body and Blood: An Interview with Martin Scorsese." *Film Comment* Oct. 1988: 36–42.

———. "A Critic's Contrarian View." *Time* 15 Aug. 1988: 36.

Corrigan, Timothy. *A Cinema without Walls.* New Brunswick, NJ: Rutgers UP, 1991.

"Crisis of Faith." Editorial. *New Statesman & Society* 26 Aug. 1988: 39.

Cross, F. L., ed. *The Oxford Dictionary of the Christian Church.* Oxford: Oxford UP, 1988.

Cunneen, Joseph. "Film and the Sacred." *Cross Currents* April 1993: 10.

Dart, John. "Some Clerics See No Evil in Temptation." *Los Angeles Times* 14 July 1988: sec. 6: 9.

———. "Church Leaders Upset at Delay in Film Screening." *Los Angeles Times* 18 June 1988: A1.

———. "Evangelical Christians Declare Holy War on 'Last Temptation'." *Sunday Star-Ledger* 17 July 1988: 13.

———. "Full Theaters, Protests Greet 'Temptation'." *Los Angeles Times* 13 Aug. 1988: sec. 1: 1.

———. "'Last Temptation' Views Still Coming In." *Los Angeles Times* 27 Aug. 1988: sec. 2: 6.

Dawes, A. "Christian Groups Blast Universal over 'Christ' Picture." *Daily Variety* 20 July 1988: 1+ [2p].

———. Brouhaha Hurls 'Christ' to Record Biz: But More Exhibs Refuse Bookings." *Daily Variety* 17 August 1988: 5.

———. "Family Group Chief Says Battle Dented 'Temptation' Take. *Daily Variety* 9 Nov. 1988: 8.

———. "'Temptation' Furor a Blessing in Disguise, Say Fundraisers." *Daily Variety* 14 Sept. 1988: 8.

———. "Clergy Nails 'Christ' and Universal." *Daily Variety* 10 Aug. 1988: 1+ [2p].

———. "Last Temptation Touches off Protests Among European Groups." *Daily Variety* 24 August 1988: 5.

———. "Loews Giveth and Carmike Taketh Away." *Daily Variety* 24 Aug. 1988: 4+.

———. "Stolen Print is Latest Chapter in the 'Last Temptation' Saga." *Daily Variety* 31 Aug. 1988: 3+.

———. "Events and People: L. T. Boycotted." *Christian Century* 2 Nov. 1988: 977.

———. "Delay in Screening Sparks Anger." *Los Angeles Times* 18 June 1988: E14.

"Demonstrators March in Protest." *UPI* [Fargo] 12 Jan. 1989, BC cycle.

Denby, David. Review. "Time on the Cross." *New York Magazine* 29 Aug. 1988: 50.

DePietro, Thomas. Interview. "Scorsese: Making Jesus Contemporary." *Christianity and Crisis* 10 Oct. 1988: 342.

Dieckmann, Katherine. Review of *The Last Temptation of Christ,* by Martin Scorsese. *Village Voice* 23 Aug. 1988: 50.

"Director Scorsese Says 'Temptation' Film His Cinematic Prayer." *New York Newsday* 1 Aug. 1988: 11.

"Director of Christ Film Says it Defends Religious Values." *Reuter's Library Report,* [Paris] 27 Oct. 1988, AM cycle.

Dobson, James. Editorial. *Focus on the Family Citizen* (Pomona, CA) Sept. 1988: 4.

Dowd, Leslie. "Christians Protest as 'Last Temptation' Opens to Packed Houses." *AP,* [New York] 12 Aug. 1988.

Duffy, Mike. "Yahoos Create Unholy Row Over Film About Christ." *Detroit Free Press* 10 Aug. 1988: 28.

Dukovic, Evelyn. "Report on July 12 Screening of The Last Temptation of Christ." *Morality in Media* 24 July 1988: 1–4.

Easton, Nina J. "'Last Temptation' Draws Mostly Sold-out Houses." Los Angeles Times 15 Aug. 1988: sec. 6: 1.

———. "Movie Critics Debate its Merit a Passionately as Religious Leaders." *Los Angeles Times* 12 Aug. 1988: sec. 6: 1.

Ebert, Roger. "Censors Should Resist 'Temptation'. *New York Post* 22 July 1988: 26–27.

Ehrenstein, David. *The Scorsese Picture.* New York: Carroll Publishing, 1992.

Emmers, Bob. "Film on Jesus Tempts Group to Boycott." *Orange County Register* 15 July 1988: B1.

Escambia County Commission. *Minutes of Meeting.* 8 Sept. 1988: 5–27.

Escambia County Ord. 88–9. Ordinance Banning the Showing of *The Last Temptation of Christ.* Escambia Co. Florida. 8 Sept. 1988.

Escambia County Ord. 88–19. Ordinance Repealing Ord. 88–9. Escambia Co. Florida. 15 Dec. 1988.

"Falwell's Invitation to 'Christ' Film Withdrawn." *New York City Tribune* 29 July 1988: C18.

Farah, Judy. "Showing for Christian Leaders: 'Last Temptation' Draws Mixed Reviews." *The Herald* 14 July 1988: 29.

"Fifth Circuit Dismisses Case Against 'Last Temptation'." *The Entertainment Litigation Reporter* 22 Oct. 1990.

"Fighting the Good Fight." Bulletin. Rosaries for Peace. July 1988.

"Film Evokes Calls for Boycott, Caution on Censorship." *United Methodist Newscope* 29 July 1988: 4.

"Film Protest Raises Questions." *The Lutheran Magazine* 7 Sept. 1988: 17.

"Film Offensive to Cuomo." *New York Times* 24 August 1988: C19.

Fish, Stanley. *There's No Such Thing as Free Speech.* New York: Oxford UP, 1994.

Flanigan, C. Clifford. "Liminality, Carnival & Social Structure." *Victor Turner and the Construction of Cultural Criticism.* Ed. Kathleen Ashly. Bloomington: Indiana Press, 1990. 42–63.

"Florida County Repeals Ordinance Banning 'The Last Temptation of Christ'." *Entertainment Law Reporter* 10.9 (1989).

Forshey, Gerald E. *American Religious and Biblical Spectaculars.* Westport, CT: Praeger, 1992.

———. "Jesus on Film." *Christian Century* 14 Sept. 1988: 801.

"Free Speech Battle Looms." *Seattle Times* 21 March 1991: A3.

"Freedom of Religion/1st Amendment/ 'The Last Temptation of Christ'." *Texas Lawyer* 8 Oct. 1990: 8.

"French Cardinal Attacks Rushdie Book as Offending the Faithful." *Reuter's Library Report* [Paris] 21 February 1989, AM cycle: 1.

Friedman, Jerome. *Blasphemy, Immorality and Anarchy.* Athens, OH: Athens Press, 1982.

Gelmis, Joseph. "One Man's Passion Play." *New York Newsday* 11 Aug. 1988: sec. 2: 4.

Girard, René. *The Scapegoat.* Trans. Yvonne Freccero, Baltimore: Johns Hopkins University Press, 1986.

————. *Things Hidden since the Foundation of the World.* Trans. Stephen Bann and Michael Metteer. Stanford, CA : Stanford UP, 1987.

Goff, Lisa, and Lewis Lazare. "Speaking Out in Favor of Temptation." *Crain's Chicago Business* 15 Aug. 1988: 8.

Gold, Richard. "N.Y. Fest Wanted 'Christ' As Opener." *Daily Variety* 3 Aug. 1988: 18.

Gorney, Cynthia. "The 'Temptation' Furor." *Washington Post* 22 July 1988: D1.

Granberry, Michael. "'Temptation': Some Resist, Others Yawn." *Los Angeles Times* 20 Aug. 1988: sec. 2: 1.

"Greb v. Universal Pictures." *States Law Week* 28 Aug. 1990: 90.

Greeley, Andrew. Review. "Blasphemy or Artistry?" *New York Times* 14 Aug. 1988: sec. 2: 22.

Grogan, David. "In the Name of Jesus." *People* 5 Aug. 1988: 40–43.

Guthman, Edward. "NEA-Granted Film Targeted by Group." *The San Francisco Chronicle* 28 March 1991: E1.

Hanrahan, John. "Queensland Becomes First Government to Ban 'Temptation'." *Variety* 12 Oct. 1988: 38.

Harmetz, A. "Film on Christ Brings out Pickets and Archbishop Predicts Censure." *New York Times* 21 July 1988: C19.

————. "How Studio Maneuvered 'Temptation' Into a Hit." *New York Times* 24 Aug. 1988: C15 + [2p].

————. "'Last Temptation' Sets a Record as Pickets Decline." *New York Times* 15 Aug. 1988: C14.

————. "Ministers Vow Boycott Over Scorsese Film on Jesus." *New York Times* 13 July 1988: C15.

————. "New Scorsese Film Shown to Religious Leaders." *New York Times* 15 July 1988: C30.

————. "Scorsese 'Temptation' Gets Early Release." *New York Times* 5 Aug. 1988: C13.

————. "7,500 Picket Universal Over Movie About Jesus." *New York Times* 12 Aug. 1988: C4.

————. "'The Last Temptation' Opens to Protests but Good Sales. *New York Times* 13 Aug. 1988: 11.

————. "Top Studios Support 'Christ' Film." *New York Times* 25 July 1988: C18.

Hinson, Hal. "The Imperfect Power of 'Temptation'; Scorsese's Flawed Epic of an Uncertain Jesus." Rev. of *The Last Temptation of Christ*, by Martin Scorsese. *Washington Post* 12 Aug. 1988: B1.

Hirath, R. H. "The Film and its Implications." *America* 20 Aug. 1988: 102+ [2p].

Hirsley, Michael. "Bishops Call: Shun 'L.T.'" *Chicago Tribune* 10 Aug. 1988, Final Edition: 12.

———. "Last Temptation Fans Swamp Foes at Theaters." *Chicago Tribune* 14 Aug. 1988, Final Edition: 3.

———. "Los Angeles Christians Protest Movie." *Chicago Tribune* 12 Aug. 1988: 5.

Hodenfield, Chris. "The Infuriating Martin Scorsese." *American Film* Mar. 1989: 46–51.

Holden, Anthony. *Behind the Oscar: The Secret History of the Academy Awards.* New York: Plume, 1993.

Hopkins, J. "Crisis of Faith." *New Statesman & Society* 26 Aug. 1988: 39.

Hudson, Ronald. Letter. "The Real Christ." *Maclean's* 5 Sept. 1988: 4.

Hunter, James Davison. *Culture Wars.* New York: Basic Books, 1990.

———. *Before the Shooting Begins: Searching for Democracy in America's Culture War.* New York: Free Press, 1994.

James, C. "Fascination with Faith Fuels Work by Scorsese." *New York Times* 8 Aug. 1988: C11+ [2p].

Jacobsen, Harlan. "You Talkin to Me?" *Film Comment* Oct. 1988: 32–34.

Johnson, Brian. "The Stormy Debate Over Jesus and Sex." *Maclean's* 15 Aug. 1988: 53.

Johnston, Philip. "BBC Drops Last Temptation film." *The Daily Telegraph* 5 Nov. 1991: 1.

Jones, Rev. Theodore. Letter. *Boston Globe* 21 Sept. 1988: 18.

"Judge Overturns Ban On Film." *New York Times* 10 Sept. 1988: sec. 1: 34.

Kaminsky, Stuart M. *American Film Genres.* Chicago: Nelson-Hall, 1986.

Kasindorf, Martin. "'Last Temptation' to Open 6 Weeks Early." *New York Newsday* 6 Aug. 1988: sec. 4: 15.

Kauffmann, Stanley. "Stanley Kauffmann on Films." Rev. of *The Last Temptation of Christ*, by Martin Scorsese. *The New Republic* 199 (1988): 28–29.

Kazantzakis, Nikos. *The Last Temptation of Christ.* Trans. P. A. Bien. New York: Simon & Schuster, 1960.

———. *Kazantzakis: A Biography Based on His Letters.* Trans. Borje Knos. New York: Simon & Schuster, 1968.

Kelly, Mary Pat. *Martin Scorsese: A Journey.* New York: Thunder's Mouth Press, 1989.

———. "Jesus Gets the Beat: An Interview with Martin Scorsese." *Commonweal* 9 Sept. 1988: 467.

Kellman, S. G. "'The Last Temptation of Christ: Blaming the Jews." *Midstream* 34 (1988): 33–37.

Keyser, Les. *Martin Scorsese.* New York: Twayne Publishers, 1995.

Keyser, Les, and Barbara Keyser. *Hollywood and the Catholic Church.* Chicago: Loyola UP, 1984.

King of Kings. Dir. Nicholas Ray. Perf. Jeffrey Hunter and Rip Torn. Metro-Goldwyn-Mayer, 1961.

Kinnard, Roy, and Tim Davis. *Divine Images: A History of Jesus on the Screen.* New York: Citadel Press, 1992.

Klawans, Stuart. "Betrayed." Rev. of *The Last Temptation of Christ,* by Martin Scorsese. *The Nation* 19 Sept. 1988: 210.

Knuffe, Christopher. "Emergency Prayer Appeal: The Drought of 1988." *Merciful Love Newsletter* 1 July 1988: 1.

Koller, Kerry J. "Why Do All the Critics Rave?" *New Heaven/New Earth.* Nov. 1988: 16–17.

Kornblit, Simon M. (Universal Studios) Letter to Evelyn Dukovic. 21 June 1988.

Kosmin, Barry A., and Seymour P. Lachman, *One Nation Under God: Religion in Contemporary American Society.* New York: Crown Trade Paperbacks, 1993.

Krauthammer, Charles. Letter. Washington Post 19 Aug. 1988: A23.

LaCamera, Kathleen. "UM Newscope." *National Weekly Newsletter for United Minister Leaders.* 29 July 1988: 1.

Lacayo, R. "Religion: Days of Ire and Brimstone." *Time* 25 July 1988: 73.

Lambert, Angela. "Was She a Saint or a Sinner?" *London Daily Mail* 22 July 1993: 13.

Last Temptation of Christ, The. Dir. Martin Scorsese. Perf. Willem Defoe, Barbara Hershey, and Harvey Keitel. Universal Studios, 1988. VHS. 165 min.

Last Temptation of Christ, The. Dir. Martin Scorsese. Perf. Willem Defoe, Barbara Hershey, and Harvey Keitel. Universal Studios, 2000. DVD. 165 min.

"'Last Temptation' Opens Amid Protests." *UPI,* [Boston] 2 Sept. 1988 BC cycle.

"'Last Temptation' Released on Home Video." *St. Louis Post-Dispatch* 30 June 1989: 4B.

"'Last Temptation' too Quickly Damned." Letter. *St. Petersburg Times* 20 Aug. 1988: 7E.

Lawton, David. *Blasphemy.* Philadelphia: U Pennsylvania P, 1993.

Lee, Robert E. A. " 'The Last Temptation of Christ,' Insulting or Instructive?" *Lutheran* 7 Sept. 1988: 15–17.

Leo, John. "A Holy Furor: Boycotts and belligerence greet a startling new film about Jesus." *Time* 15 Aug. 1988: 34–36.

Levy, Lawrence. *Blasphemy.* New York: Knopf, 1993.

Lindlof, Thomas R. "Communities out of Conflict: The Case of Scorsese's 'The Last Temptation of Christ'." SCA Convention. Hilton Hotel, New Orleans. 19 Nov. 1994.

Lipson, Karin. "The Jewish Role in Hollywood." *New York Newsday* 7 Dec. 1990: pt. 2: 96.

Lopate, Philip. Film Review: Fourteen Koans by a Levite on Scorsese's 'Last Temptation of Christ'." *Tikkun* 6 Nov. 1988: 74–78.

Lyons, Charles. "The Paradox of Protest: American Film, 1980—1992." *Movie Censorship and American Culture.* Ed. Francis G. Couvares. Washington, DC: Smithsonian Institution P, 1996. 277–318.

MacNeil/Lehrer News Hour. Public Broadcasting System. KQUED, San Francisco. 16 Aug. 1988.

Malone, Peter. *Movie Christs and Antichrists.* New York: Crossroads, 1990.

Marcuse, Herbert. *One-Dimensional Man: Studies in the Ideology of Advanced Industrial Society.* Boston: Beacon Press, 1992.

Martz, Larry. "TV Preachers on the Rocks." *Newsweek* 11 July 1988: 26–28.

Maslin, Janet. Review " 'Last Temptation': Scorsese's View of Jesus' Sacrifice." *New York Times* 12 Aug. 1988: C8.

Mason, Marilynne S. Review of "Seeing is Believing." *Christian Century* 17 July 1996: 727.

Massachusetts. *Annotated Laws of Massachusetts.* Blasphemy Stat. C.272 Sec. 36. Boston: Lawyers Cooperative Publishing 1992: 343.

Master Media Inc. Advertisement. *Hollywood Reporter* 7 July 1988: 20.

Master Media Inc. Advertisement. *Hollywood Reporter* 20 July 1988: 16.

McCabe, Jim. Letter. " 'Last Temptation' Too Quickly Damned" *St. Petersburg Times* 20 Aug. 1988: 7E.

McDonnel, Joan. "Live Wire." *Seattle Times* 19 Aug. 1988: D3.

McGrady, Mike. Review, "The Last Temptation of Christ." *New York Newsday* 12 Aug. 1988: 3.

McWilliams, Michael. "Religious Wrath: Hell Hath no Fury Like a Christian Scorned." *Playboy* Dec. 1989: 46.

Medhurst, Martin. "Temptation as Taboo: A Psychoanalytic Reading of *The Last Temptation of Christ.* " Unpublished essay, 1993.

Medved, Michael. *Hollywood VS. America.* New York: HarperCollins, 1992.

———. "Hollywood's Poison Factory: The Movies' Twisted Image." *USA Today* 18 Sept. 1993: 79.

Meredith, Lawrence. "The Gospel According to Kazantzakis: How Close Did Scorsese Come?" *Christian Century* 14 Sept. 1988: 799.

Miles, Margaret R. *Seeing and Believing: Religion and Values in the Movies.* Boston: Beacon Press, 1996.

Miller, William. *Humiliation.* Ithaca, NY: Cornell UP, 1993.

Mitchell, Elvis. "Movies and TV: Jesus Christ Movie Star." *Rolling Stone* 22 Sept. 1988: 42.

Modderno, Craig. "Theaters May Shun 'Temptation'." *Los Angeles Times* 15 July 1988: sec. 6: 8.

Monaco, James. *American Film Now: The People, the Power, the Money, the Movies.* New York: Oxford UP, 1979.

Moore, Paul. "'Last Temptation' Not Heretical." *Witness* Oct. 1988: 12–13.

"More 'Temptation' in the Bookstores." *Seattle Times* 18 Sept. 1988: K9.

Morgan, Robert C. Review. "New York in Review." *Arts Magazine* 8 Dec. 1988: 103.

Morris, Michael. "Of God and Man." *American Film* 14 Oct. 1988: 18–24.

Morris, Thomas. "Theologizing in the Public Arena." *Chicago Tribune* 27 Aug. 1988, Final Edition: 13C.

Morton, Gary. "Temptations of Flesh Bedevil 'Last Temptation'". *Florida Catholic* 29 July 1988: 33.

"MPAA Supports U's 'Temptation'." *Daily Variety* 27 July 1988: 3–4.

Muck, Terry. Editorial. "Holy Indignation." *Christianity Today* 16 Sept. 1988: 18.

Nayeri, Farah. "'Temptation' Galls Gallic Groups; Fracases at Several French Sites." *Daily Variety* 5 Oct. 1988: 23.

———. "Paris Sites Drop Film After Protester Assaults." *Daily Variety* 19 Oct. 1988: 481.

Nassif, Bradley. "Heresy in the Early Church." *Christian History* 51. 15. 3 (1996): 20–36.

Neff, David. "Scorsese's Christ." Letter. *Christianity Today* 7 Oct. 1988: 12–13.

Nelson, Don. "Universal Succumbs to 'Temptation'" *New York Daily News* 15 Aug. 1988: 28.

Oeglaend, Margarete. *Martin Scorsese: God's Lonely Man.* Master's Thesis. California State U, 1991. Ann Arbor, UMI, 1991.

"Oklahoma State University group seeks damages." *The Entertainment Law Reporter* 14.6 (1992): 2.

Oney, Steve. "The Forces that Fired 'Last Temptation'; Martin Scorsese: The Payoff for a Director's Dedication." *Washington Post* 14 Aug. 1988: G1.

"Opponents Are Undeterred as the Multitudes Flock to 'Last Temptation'." *Chicago Tribune* 16 August 1988: 14.

Oprah Winfrey Show, The. Host, Oprah Winfrey. CBS. WCBS, New York. 16 Aug. 1988.

Ostrum, Carol M. "Scripts VS Scripture." *Seattle Times* 11 Aug. 1988: G1.

"Oz Censors Lower Classification on 'Temptation': Protests Arise." *Daily Variety* 19 Oct. 1988: 481.

"Peaceful, Prayerful Protest Rally Opposes Opening of L.T.'" *Southwest Wire,* [Dallas] 31 Aug. 1988: 1.

Pede, R. "The Last Temptation of Christ." *Film and Television* Fall 1988: 8–12.

Poland, Larry. *The Last Temptation of Hollywood.* Highland, CA: Mastermedia International, 1988.

Pollock, J. "St. Louisans Finally Seeing 'Christ', But Not Sans Incident." *Daily Variety* 5 Oct. 1988: 23.

Pomponio, Faith. (Morality in Media) Letter to Simon Kornblit. 23 June 1988.

Pond, Steve. "1988: The Films and the Flaps." *Washington Post* 30 Dec. 1988: G7.

Powers, Stephen, et al. *Hollywood's America: Social and Political Themes in Motion Pictures.* Boulder, CO: Westview Press, 1996.

"Protests, False Bomb Threat over Movie." *United Press International* [Seattle] 30 May 1989, BC cycle.

Pryor, T. M. "'Christ' Protesters Should Save Their Ammo until Picture Opens." *Daily Variety* 20 July 1988: 8.

Pugh, Jeanne. "'Last Temptation' While Not Pretty, is Dynamic, Moving." Review of *The Last Temptation of Christ,* by Martin Scorsese. *St. Petersburg Times* 10 September 1988: 1E.

Quinn, John. "K.C. Gets Share of Protesters as Pic Plays One Site." *Daily Variety* 5 Oct. 1988: 23.

Ray, Robert. *A Certain Tendency in Hollywood Cinema, 1930–1980.* Princeton, NJ: Princeton UP, 1985.

Rabey, Steve. "Producer Tries to Dim Fears over Movie." *Christianity Today* 4 March 1988: 43.

Raybin, David. "Aesthetics, Romance and Turner." *Victor Turner and the Construction of Cultural Criticism.* Ed. Kathleen Ashly. Bloomington: Indiana UP, 1990. 21–41.

Reilly, Joseph. Letter to Constituents. "Last Temptation, A Partial Post-Mortem." *Morality in Media Newsletter* 8 Sept. 1988.

"Religion: Nayak v. MCA Inc." *States Law Week* 22 Jan. 1991: 90–139.

"Resisting Temptation." Narr. Jeffrey Kaye. *MacNeil/Lehrer News Hour.* PBS. WGBH, Boston. 14 Aug. 1988. Trans. 3238:17.

Robbins, J. "NATO Newsletter Resumes With Policy on 'Christ', Other Issues." United Press International 5 Oct. 1988: 23.

———. "Brouhaha Hurls 'Christ' to Record Biz." *Daily Variety* 17 Aug. 1988: 5 + [2p].

———. "'Last Temptation' War Rages on: Exhibitors Pressured." *Daily Variety* 3 Aug. 1988: 6.

Rosenbaum, Jonathan. Review of *The Last Temptation of Christ,* by Martin Scorsese. *Sight & Sound* Autumn 1988: 281.

Rothman, Stanley. "Is God Really Dead in Beverly Hills?: Religion and the Movies." *American Scholar* Spring 1996: 272.

Rueckert, William H. *Encounters with Kenneth Burke.* Urbana: U of Illinois P, 1994.

———. *Kenneth Burke and the Drama of Human Relations.* Minneapolis: U of Minnesota P, 1963.

———. "Rereading K. Burke: Doctrine Without Dogma, Action with Passion." *The Legacy of Kenneth Burke.* Madison: U of Wisconsin P, 1989. 239–262.

Ryan, James. "Scorsese's Oscar Nomination Was Act of Faith in Him." *United Press International* [New York] 30 Mar. 1989, BC cycle.

Schrader, Paul. *Schrader on Schrader.* Ed. David Thompson and Ian Christie. Boston: Faber & Faber, 1989.

———. "The Last Temptation of Christ." Unpublished Screenplay, June 1986.

Scorsese, Martin. Interview with David Rensin. *Playboy* April 1991: 57.

Scorsese, Martin. *Scorsese on Scorsese*. Ed. David Thompson and Ian Christie. Boston: Faber and Faber, 1989.

"Scorsese Firm on 'Temptation'" *Daily Variety* 27 July 1988: 26.

"Scorsese Picture Center of Holy War." *Daily Variety* 27 July 1988: 26.

"Scuffle Breaks out During 'Last Temptation' Protest." *Los Angeles Times* 5 Sept. 1988: sec. 6: 12.

Shafer, Ingrid. "The Catholic Imagination in Popular Film and Television." *Journal of Popular Film & Television* 19 Summer 1991: 50–57.

Shaffer, Gina. "200 Rally at Universal Studios to Protest Movie About Jesus." *New York Daily News* 17 July, 1988: 6.

Shaffer, Thomas. "The Tension Between Law in America and the Religious Tradition." *The Weightier Matters of the Law: Essays on Law and Religion*. Edited John Witte. Atlanta: Scholar's Press, 1988. 315–36.

Sharrett, Christopher. "The Last Temptation of Christ." *Cineaste* 17. 1 (1989): 28.

Siskel, Gene. "'Last Temptation' One of the Finest Religious Films Ever." Rev. of *The Last Temptation of Christ* by Martin Scorsese. *Chicago Tribune* 12 Aug. 1988: A.

———. "Scorsese's Temptation." *Chicago Tribune* 14 Aug. 1988, sec. 13: 4.

Smith, Lori J. "Willem Dafoe and Scorsese's Temptation." *American Film* Oct. 1988: 52.

Sobran, Joseph. "Jesus, We Hardly Knew Ye." *National Review* 16 Sept. 1988: 30–32.

Stallybrass, Peter, and Allon White. *The Politics and Poetics of Transgression*. Ithaca, NY: Cornell UP, 1986.

Tatum, W. Barnes. *Jesus at the Movies: A Guide to the First Hundred Years*. Santa Rosa, CA: Polebridge Press, 1997.

Tallmer, Jerry. Review, "The Last Temptation of Christ." *New York Post* 12 Aug. 1988: 21.

"'Temptation' Protest Leads to Slashing of Athens Screens." *Daily Variety* 19 Oct. 1988: 481.

"'Temptation' Banned For Month In Greece." *Daily Variety* 30 Nov. 1988: D3.

Thieman, Ronald F. *Religion in Public Life: A Dilemma for Democracy*. Georgetown: Georgetown UP, 1996.

Thomas, Cal. Editorial. "Cal Thomas on 'Christ' Film." *Los Angeles Times* 23 Aug. 1988: sec. 2. 6.

"Three Local Movie Chains Likely to Pass on 'Temptation'." *UPI* [Baltimore] 11 Aug. 1988 BC cycle.

Tortorano, David. "Judge Blocks County Ban of 'Temptation'." *UPI* [Miami] 9 Sept. 1988, AM cycle.

Tunstall, Jeremy, and David Walker. *Media Made in California: Hollywood, Politics and the News*. New York: Oxford UP, 1981.

Turner, Victor, and Edith Turner. *Image and Pilgrimage in Christian Culture*. New York: Columbia UP, 1978.

Turner, Victor. *The Ritual Process: Structure and Anti-structure.* Chicago: Aldine Publishing, 1969.

———. *Dramas, Fields and Metaphors: Symbolic Action in Human Society.* Ithaca, NY: Cornell UP, 1974.

———. *From Ritual to Theater: The Human Seriousness of Play.* New York: PAJ Publications, 1982.

"Uncertain Future for 'Temptation' in Brazil." *Daily Variety* 14 Sept. 1988: 8.

"Universal City, Calif—'Last Temptation' Released on Video." *St. Louis Post Dispatch* 30 June 1989: 4B.

Universal Studios. Advertisement. *New York Times* 15 July 1988: C17.

Universal Studios Press Kit on *The Last Temptation of Christ.* Universal Studios, July 1988.

"U.S. Supreme Court Refuses to Bar 'Last Temptation of Christ'." *The Entertainment Litigation Reporter* 11.9 (1990).

"U.S. Catholic Bishops Denounce Movie." *Daily Progress* 20 Aug. 1988: B4.

Voland, John. "Morning Report: Movies." *Los Angeles Times* 9 Nov. 1988: sec. 6:2.

Wall, James. "'Temptation a Failure." *Christian Century* 10 Aug. 1988: 14.

Walsh, Frank. *Sin and Censorship: The Catholic Church and the Motion Picture Industry.* New Haven, CT: Yale UP, 1995.

Wehling, Robert. "To Bill Bright." The Proctor & Gamble Company. 9 Jan. 1989.

White, Gayle. "Planned Early Release of 'Temptation' Deepens Christian Anger." *Atlanta Journal and Constitution* 6 Aug. 1988: B1.

Wildmon, Donald. Editorial. *American Family Journal* 15 June 1988: 7.

———. Editorial. *American Family Journal.* 15 July 1988: 1.

———. Editorial. *American Family Journal.* 1 Sept. 1988.

Williamson, Bruce. "Sex in Cinema 1988." *Playboy* Nov. 1988: 132.

Willman, Chris. "Messiah Without a Cause." Rev. of *The Last Temptation of Christ,* by Martin Scorsese. *Los Angeles Times* 21 Aug. 1988: Calendar 2.

Wilmington, Michael. "More Favorite Fiims of 1988." *Los Angeles Times* 1 Jan. 1989: Calendar 26.

Wills, Garry. "In Praise of Censure." *Time* Magazine 31 July 1989: 71.

"Whose Jesus?" Editorial. *Commonweal* 115 (1988): 483.

Wright, Chapin. "Scorsese's Kin Receives Odd Package." *New York Newsday* 23 Aug. 1988: 28.

York, Frank. "'The Last Temptation' Is a Box Office Flop." *Focus on the Family Citizen* 16 Nov. 1988: 1–2.

"Zefferelli Protests 'Temptation of Christ'." *New York Times* 9 Aug. 1988: sec. 6: 18.

INDEX

About the Author

ROBIN RILEY is Assistant Professor of Electronic Media in the College-Conservatory of Music at the University of Cincinnati.